AF446676

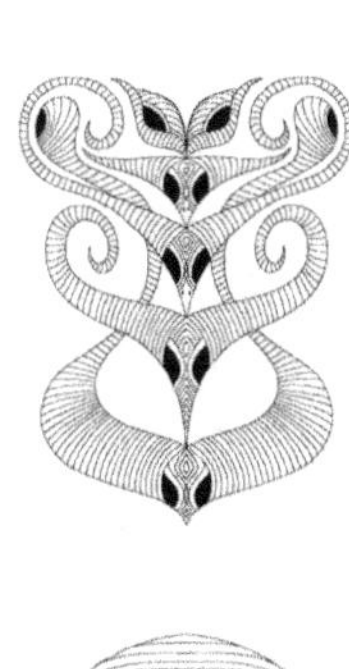
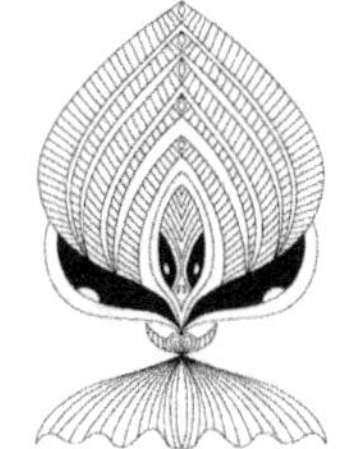
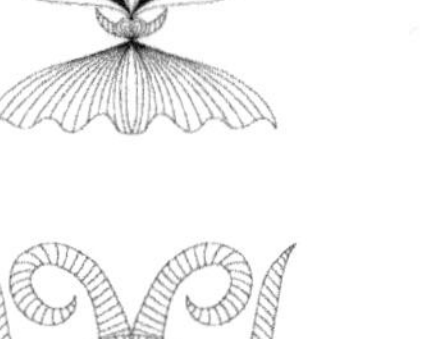

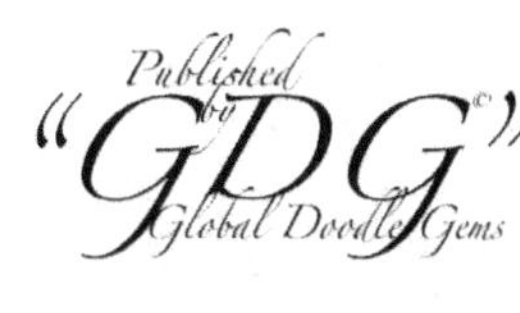

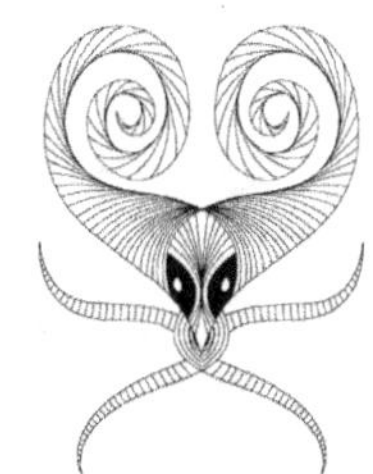

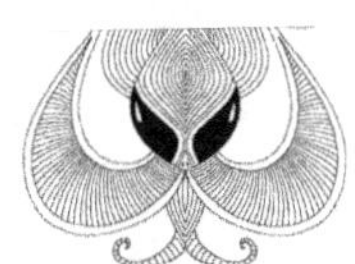

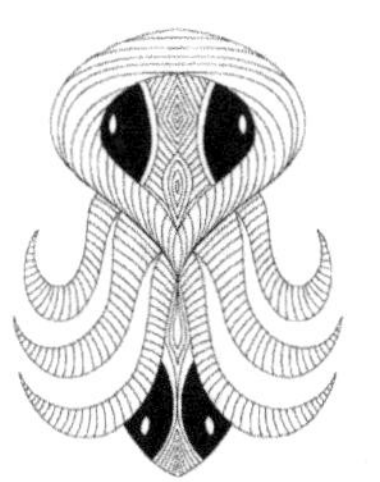
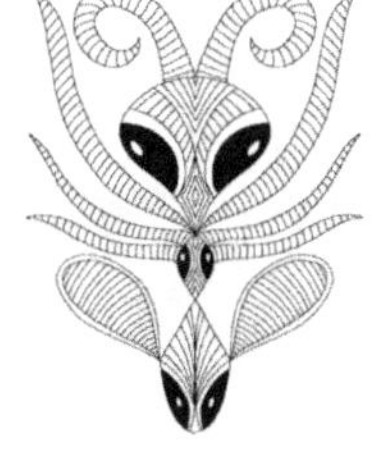
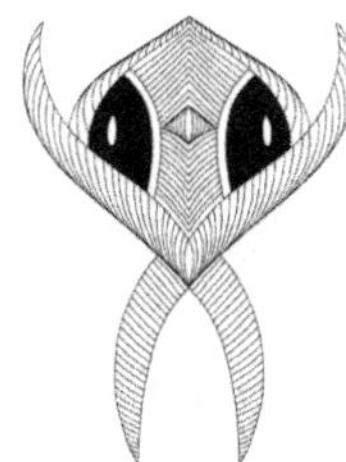
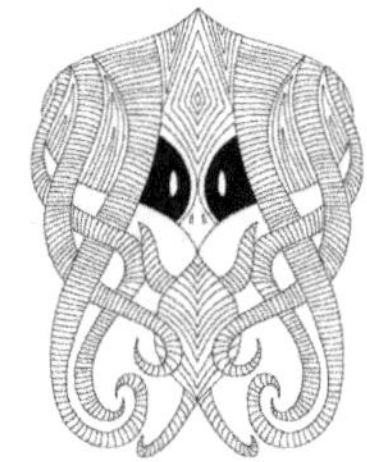
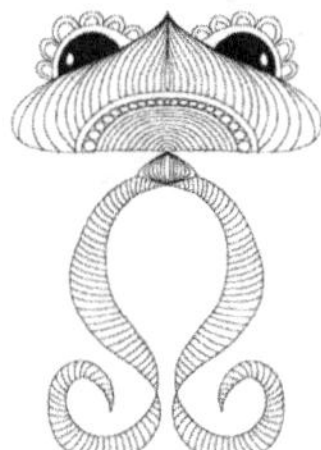

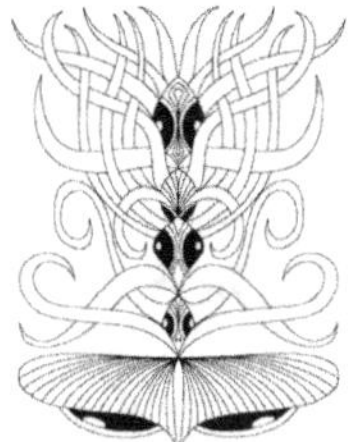
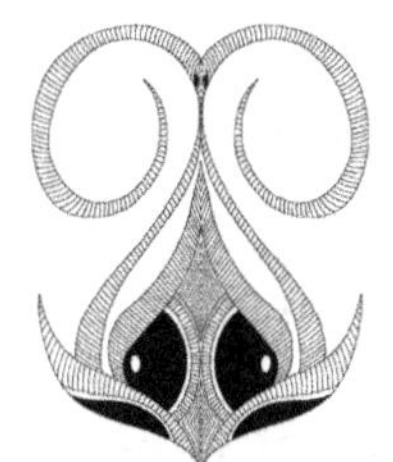
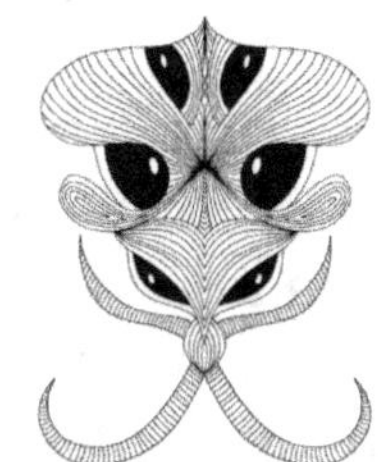
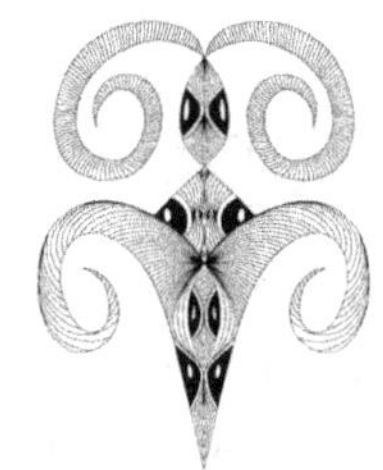
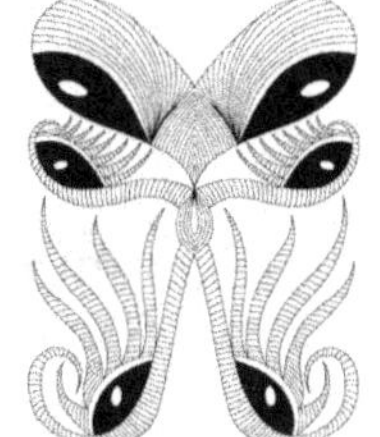

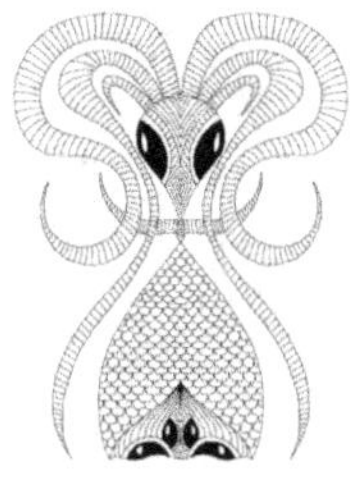

These Weirdie's
belong to the collection
of

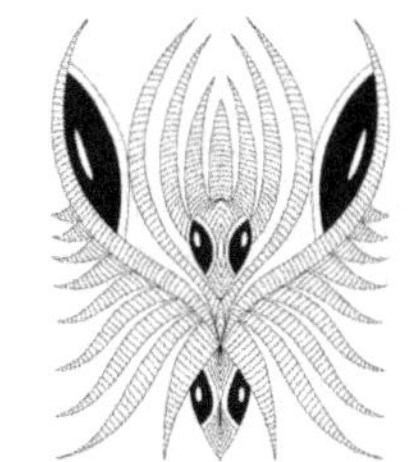

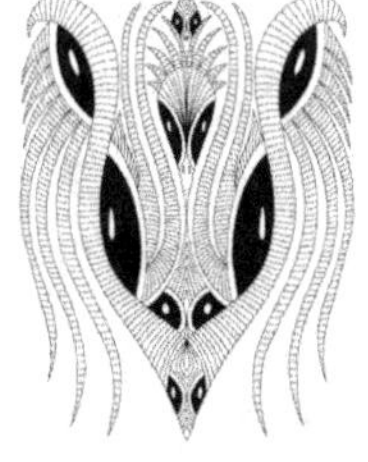
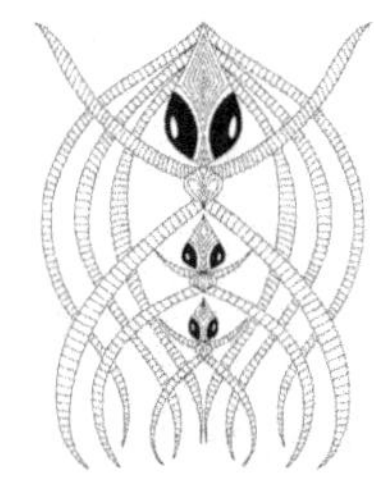
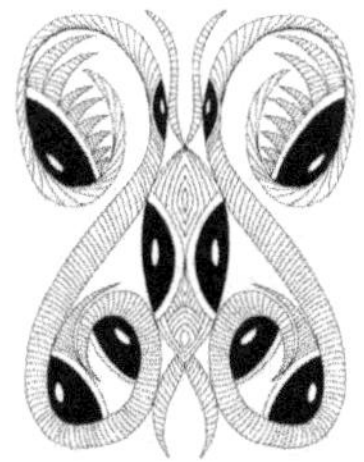
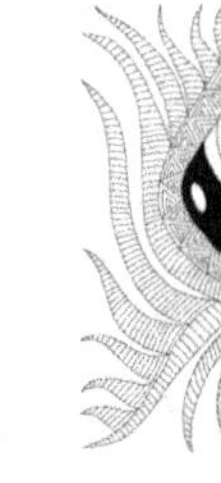
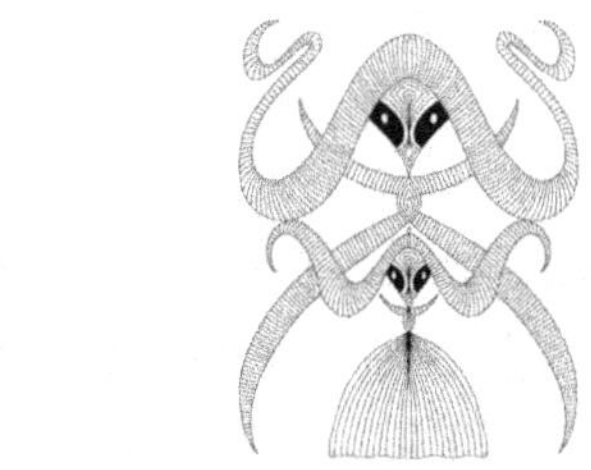

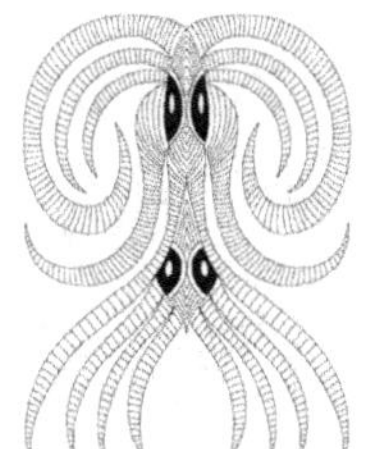
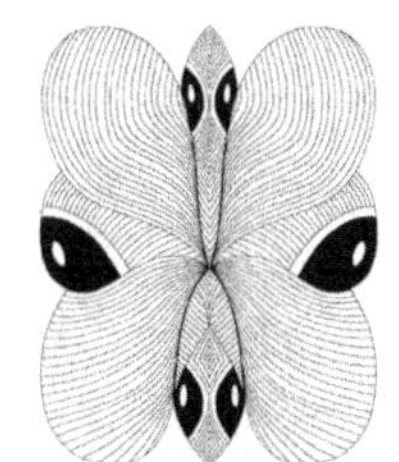
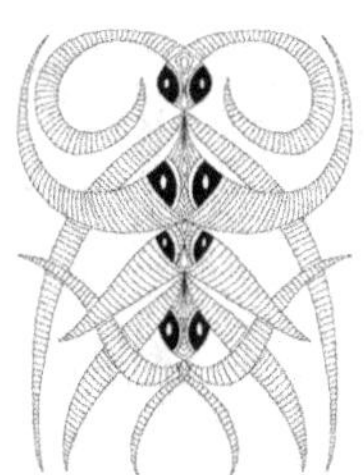
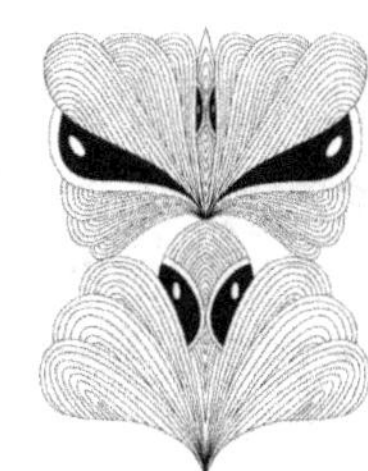
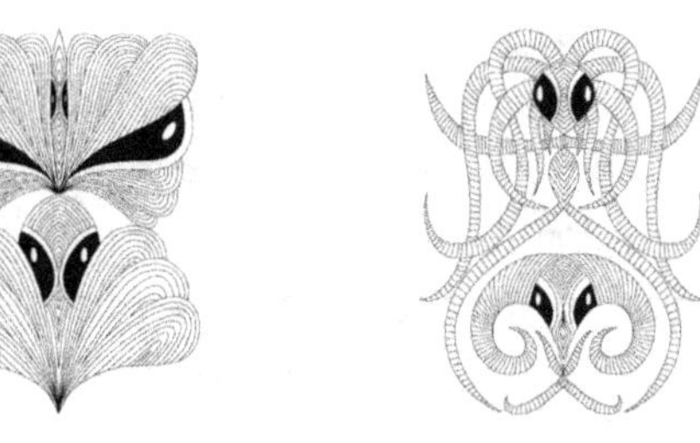

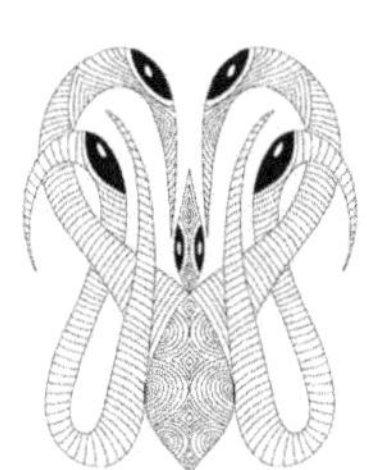
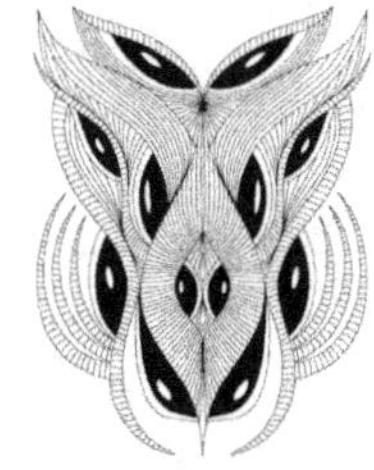
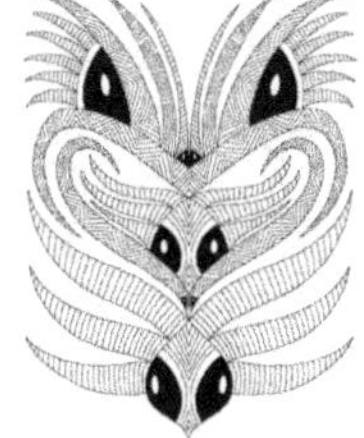
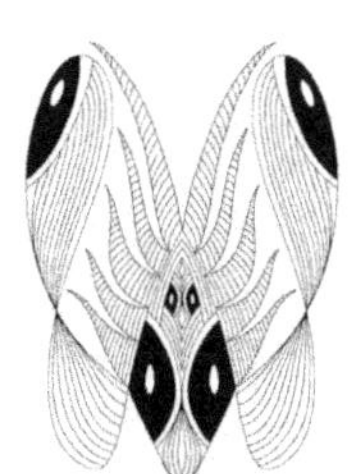
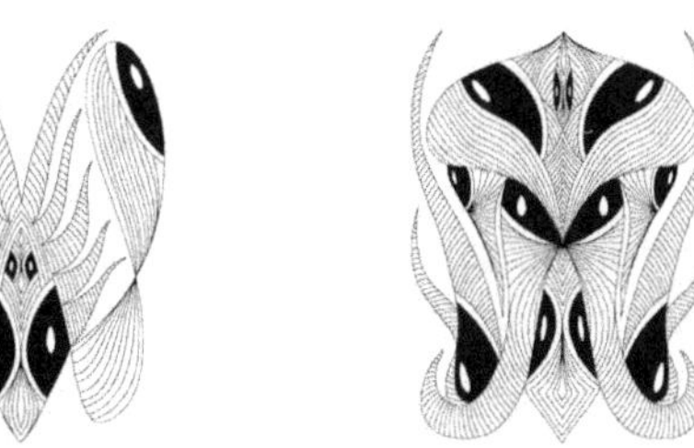

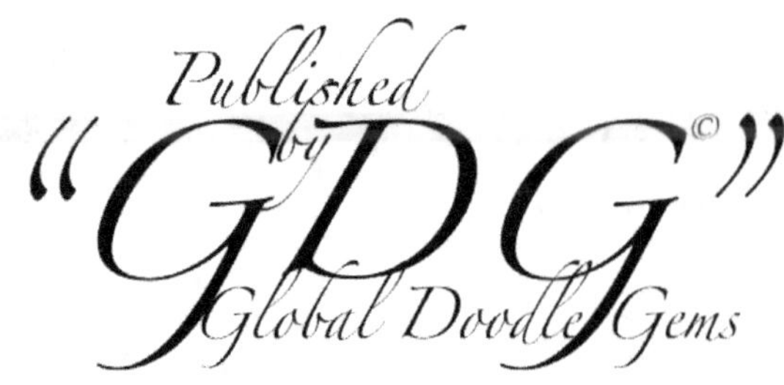

Share your colored versions with us ! We love seeing your results
and hearing from you
we are social !

The Official FB book page, stay on top of what we have in the works !
www.facebook.com/AMVWART
The Community group, share your colored pages, meet the artists, enjoy exclusive freebies, take
part in community Charity books and so much more......
www.facebook.com/groups/ColorAWeirdieADay
Follow us on Twitter.... @GlobalDoodlegem
We are on Instagram too
@globaldoodlegems for instagram
...and if you are not social like that we have a blog
globaldoodlegems.wordpress.com

Copyright © 2020 Global Doodle Gems
All rights are reserved by Global Doodle Gems.
Duplication of pages for personal use are allowed. You are invited to color the pages then scan/post
your coloured versions to social networks, mentioning the book title and author/artist (Global Doodle
Gems/Maria Wedel).
All artwork and images are protected by copyright laws. This book or any portion thereof may not,
otherwise, be reproduced and/or distributed or transmitted without the express written permission of
the artist/publisher of Global Doodle Gems.
All of us from the Global Doodle Gems wish you a colortastic time and look forward to seeing your
wonderful color results online !

Welcome to my world of Weirdies

This is the third weirdies book of year 5 of Color A Weirdie A Day,
join us for daily coloring with either me or one of the wonderful guesthosts
at the group www.facebook.com/groups/ColorAWeirdieADay,
and check out all the beautiful colored !
The set has 12 books Weirdies 49 to Weirdies 60, one book for each month
with a Weirdie for each day, additionally all Weirdies are repeated in the
back of the book in their upside_down versions ...
Your Weirdie can drastically change and turn in to a brand new Weirdie.
Get your Weirdie on and have a fun and relaxing time with coloring it,
join the group and show your colored, join the live coloring and have fun
with us ... if you like !
Weirdies 1 to 12 were colored live in 2018 Weirdies 13 to 24 were colo-
red live in 2019 Weirdies 25 to 36 were colored 2020 and Weirdies 37
to 48 were colored in 2021

Weirdies 49 will be colored in January 2022 Daily
Weirdies 50 will be colored in February 2022 Daily
Weirdies 51 will be colored in March 2022 Daily

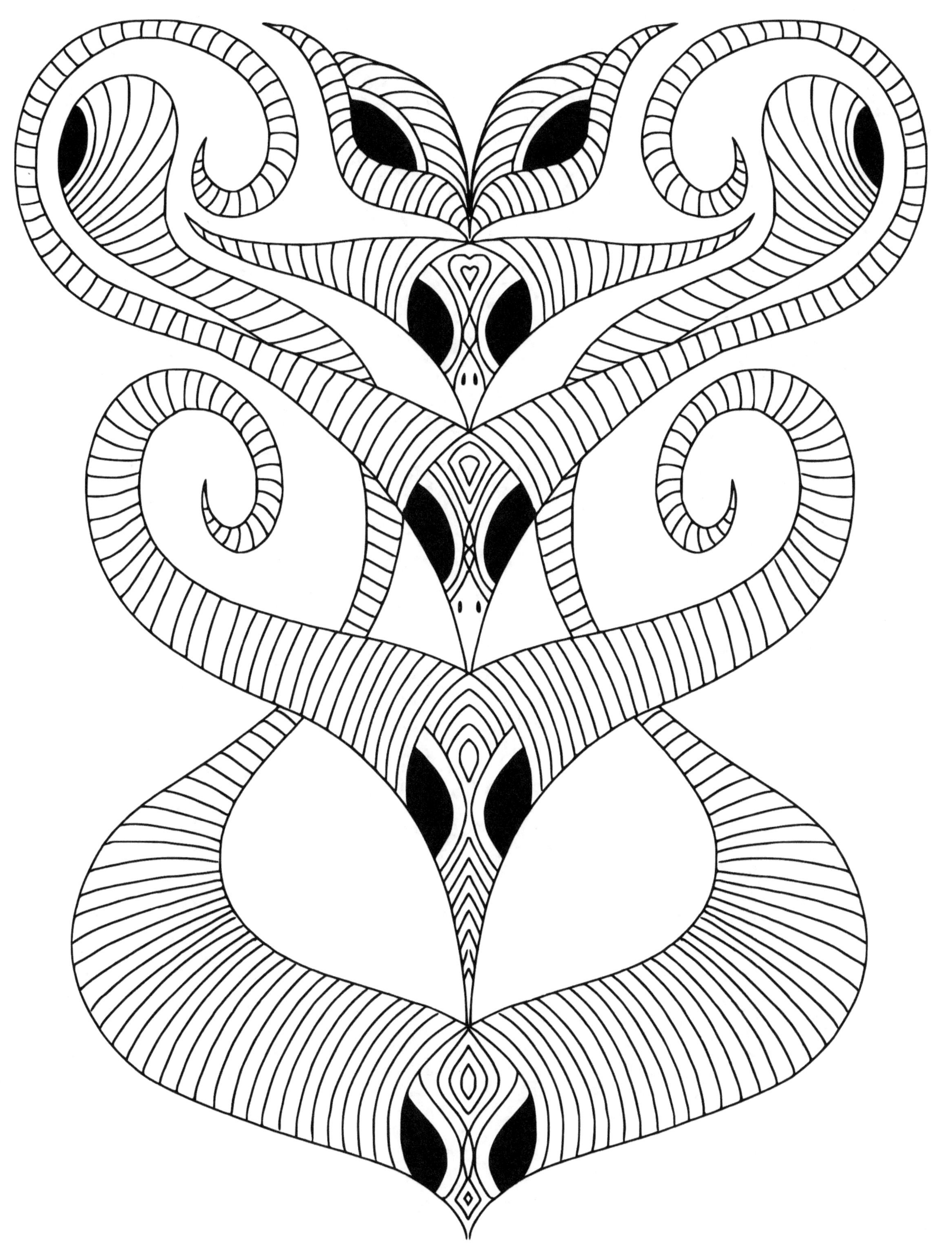

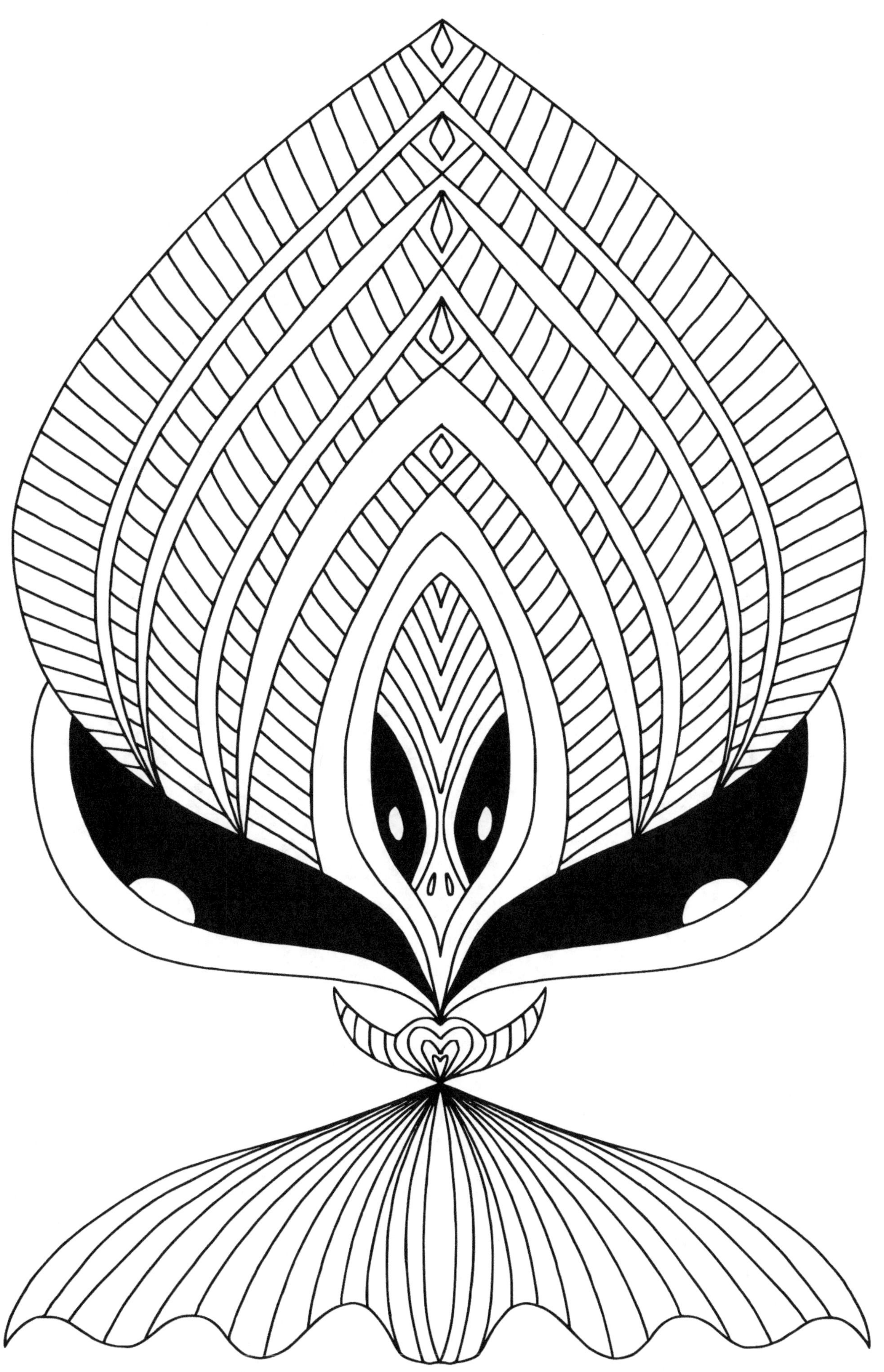

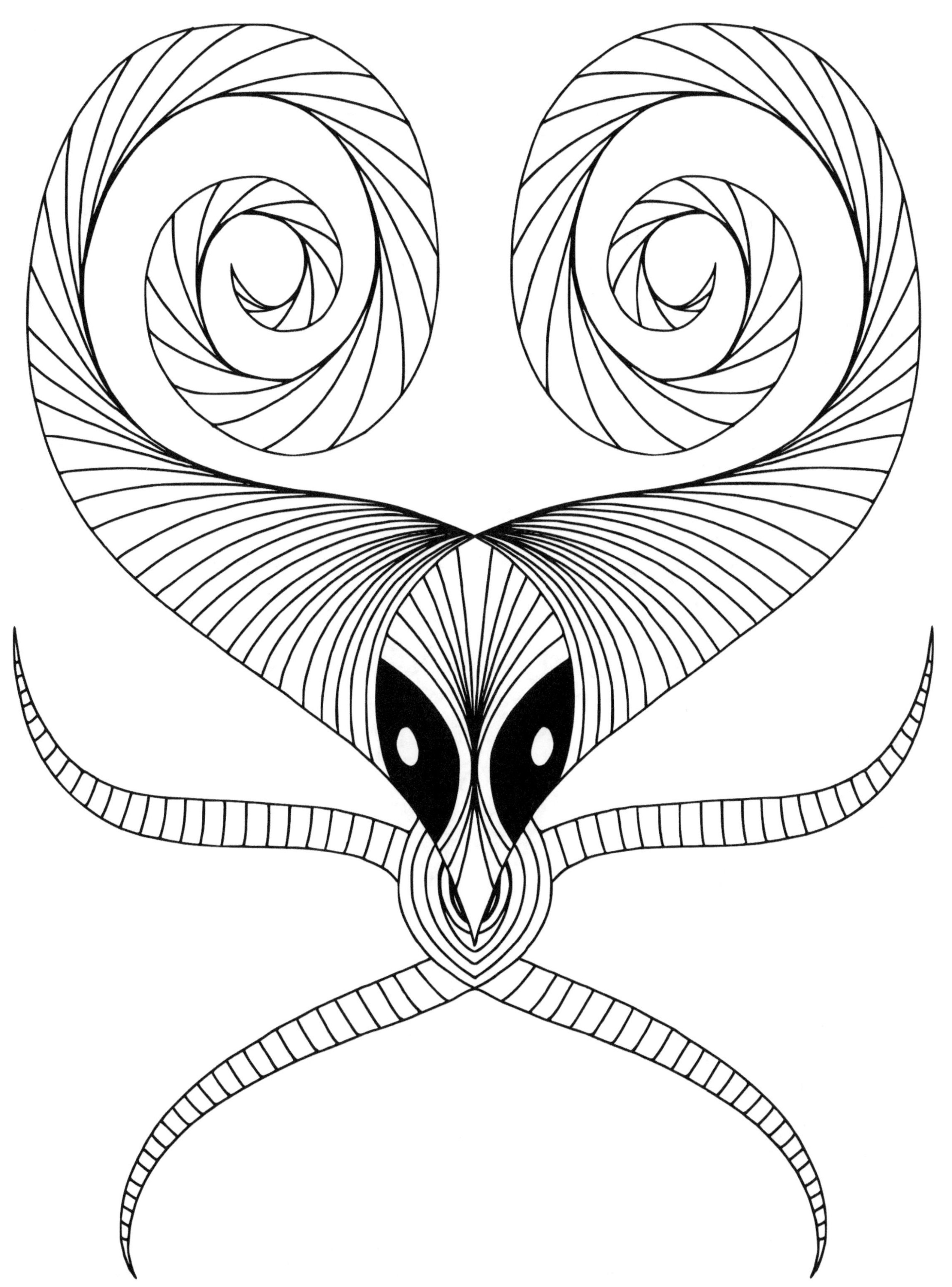

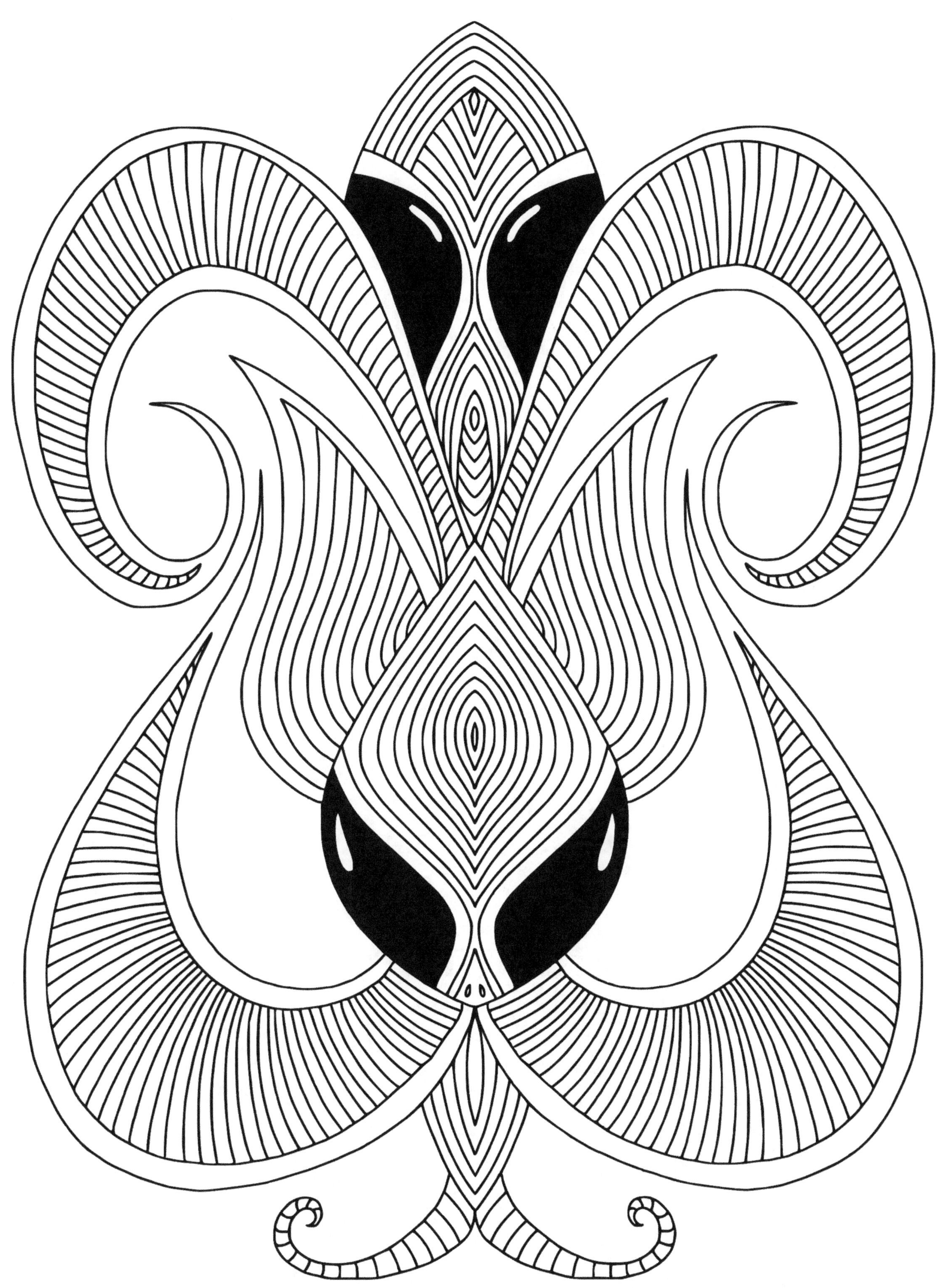

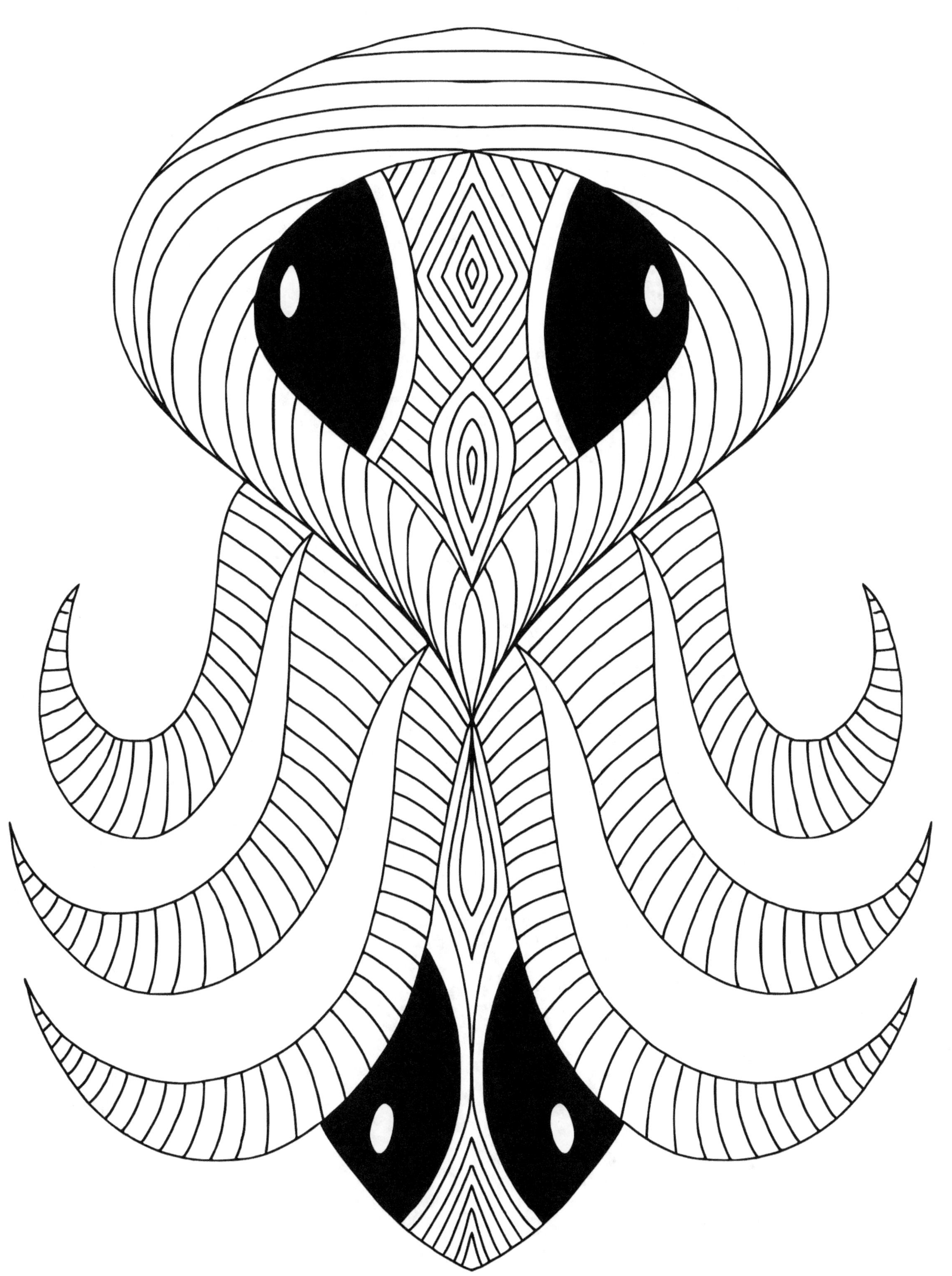

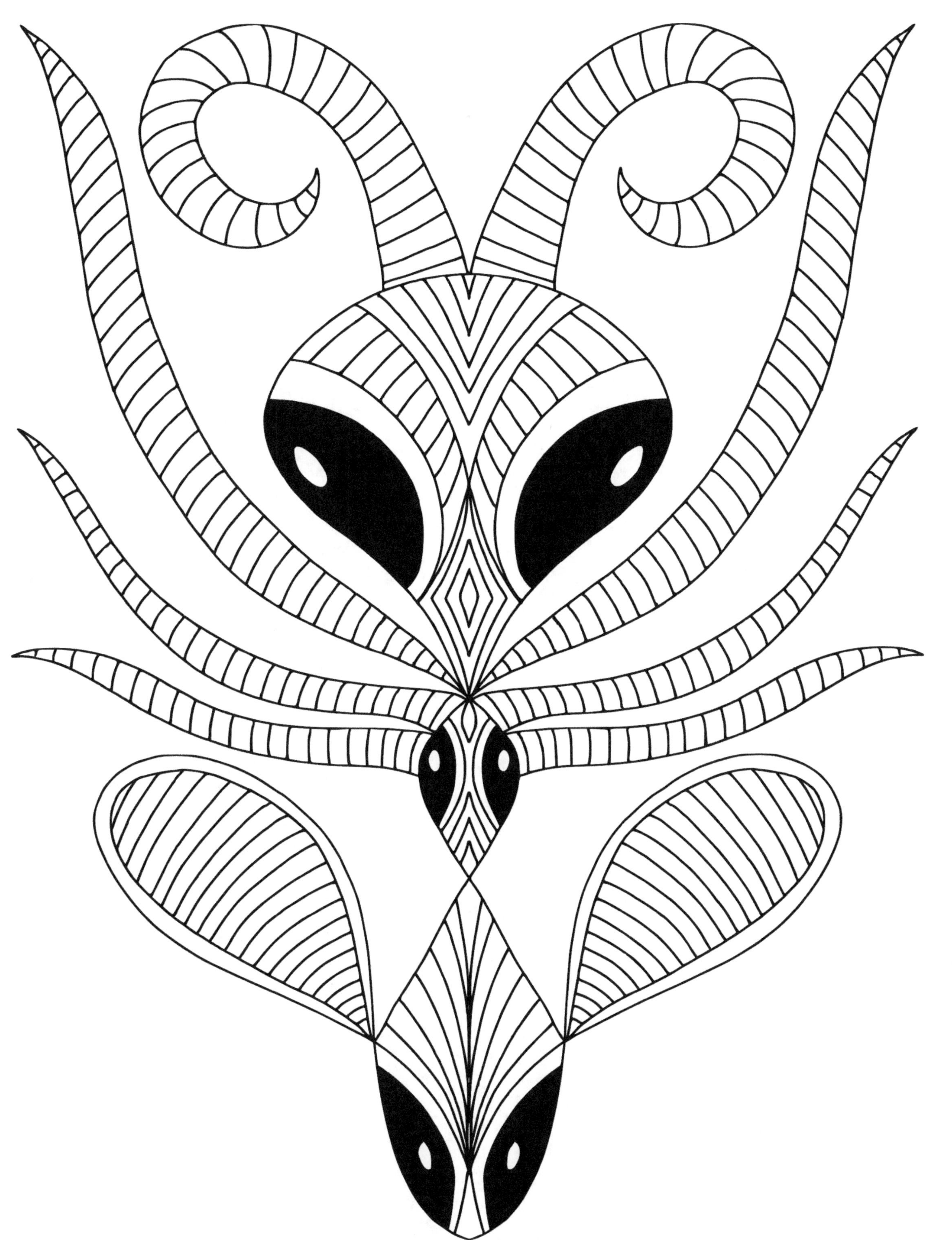

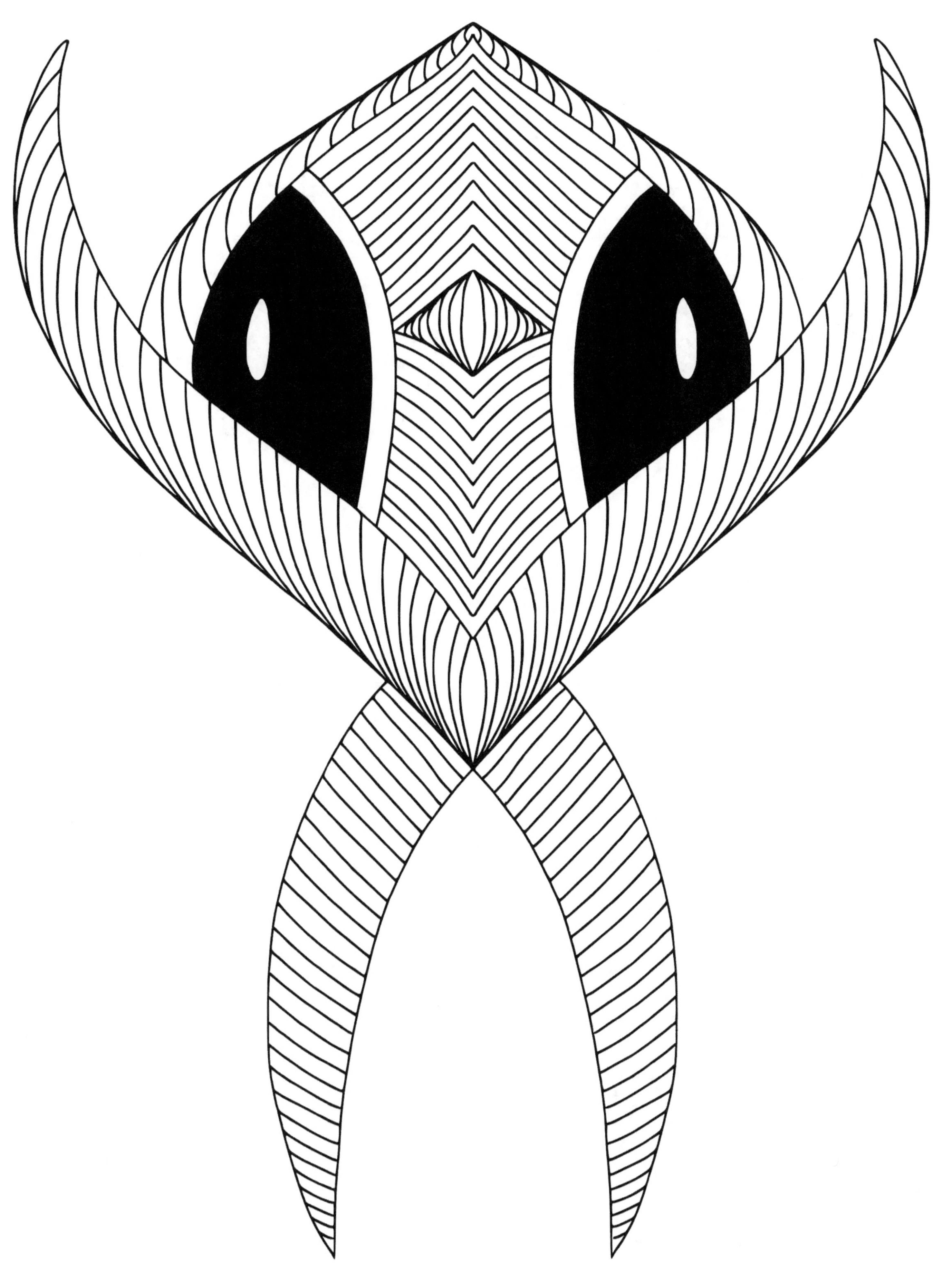

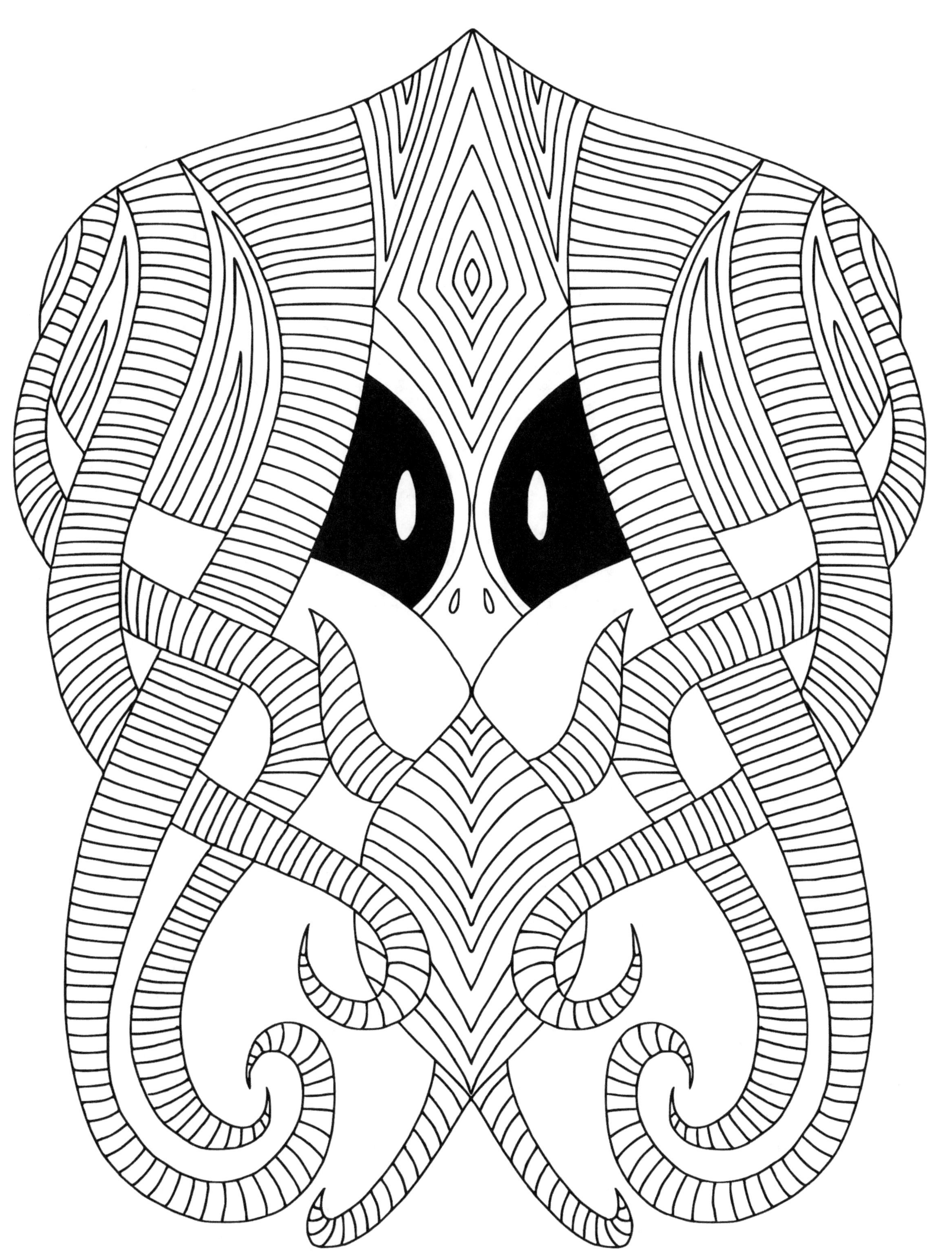

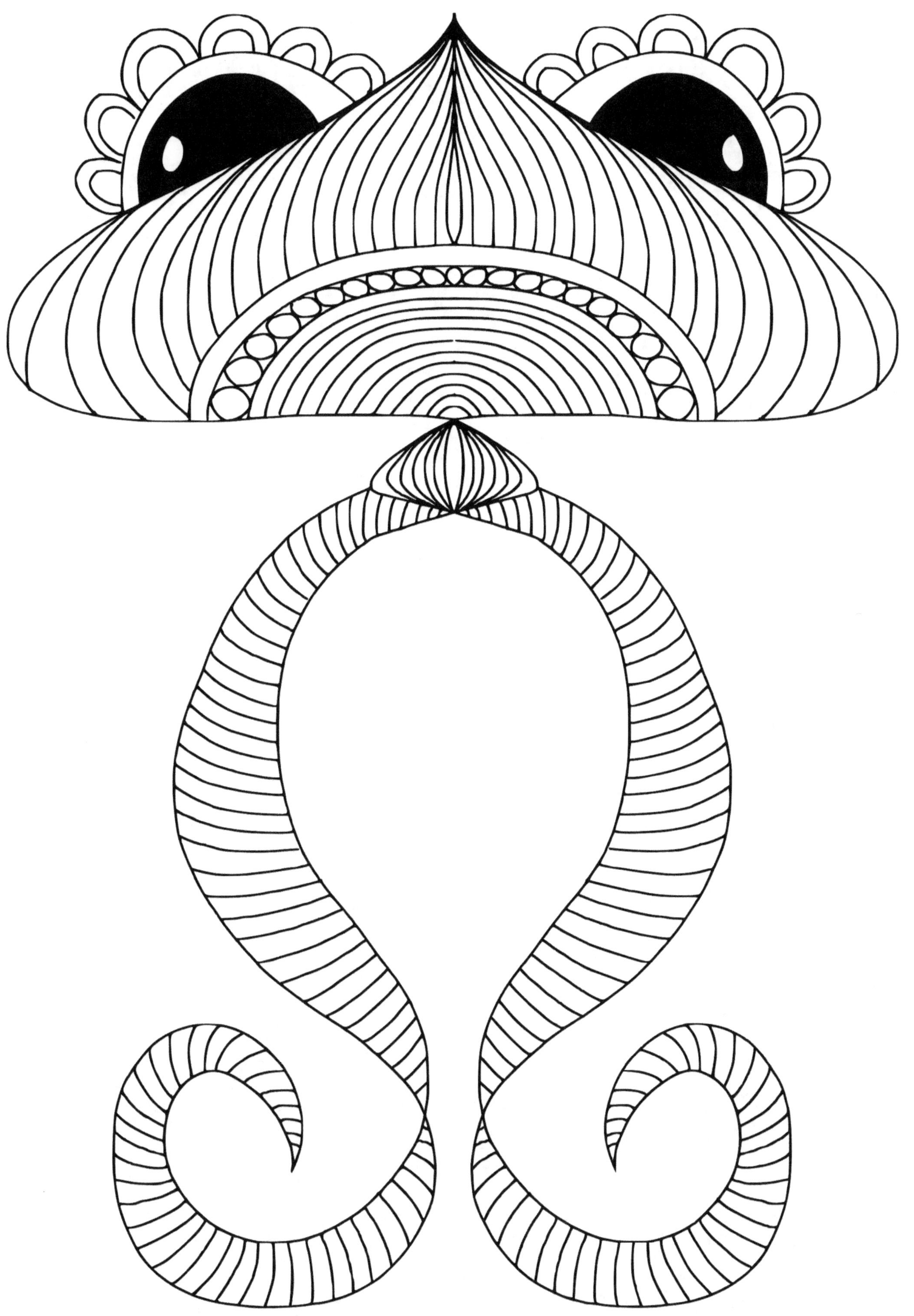

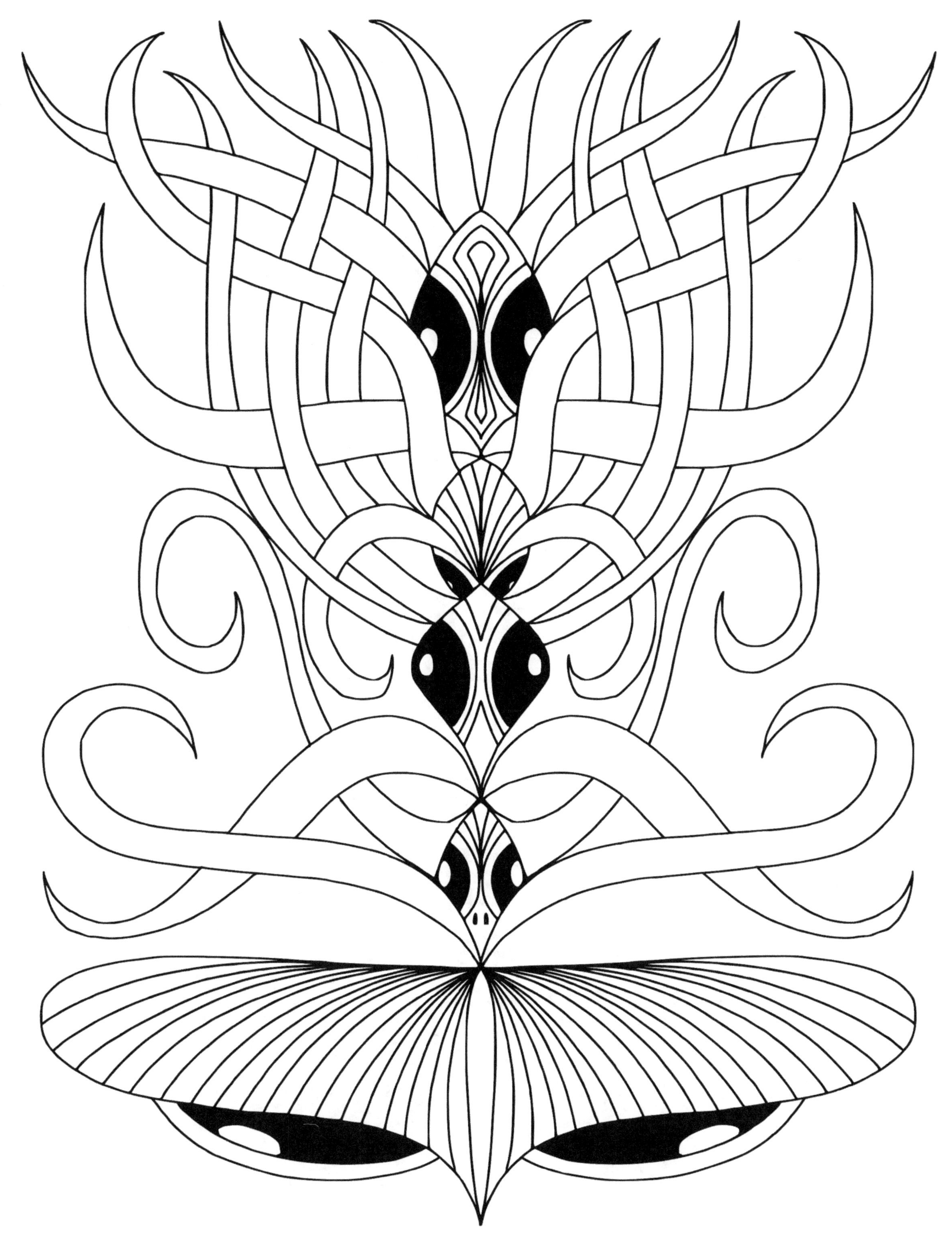

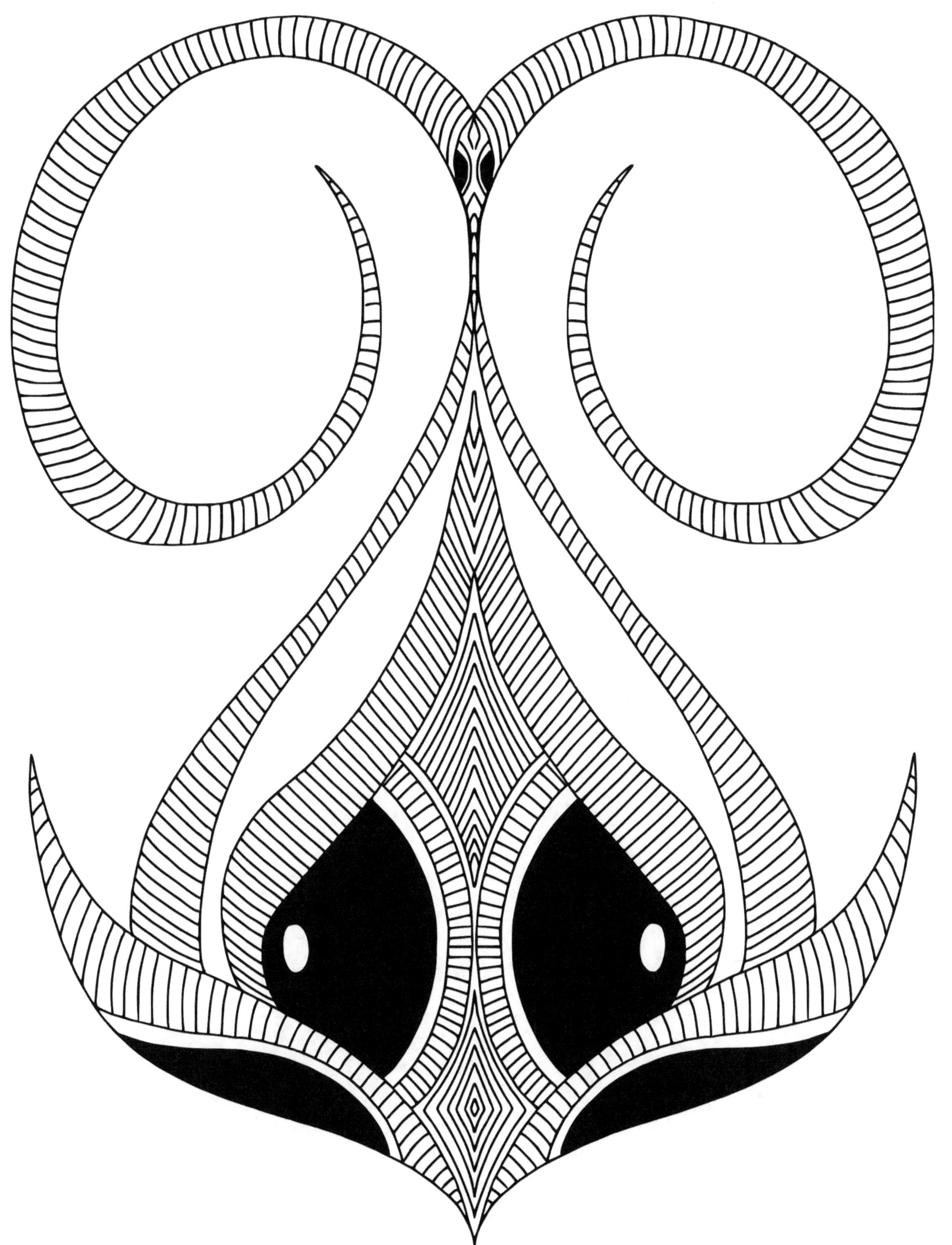

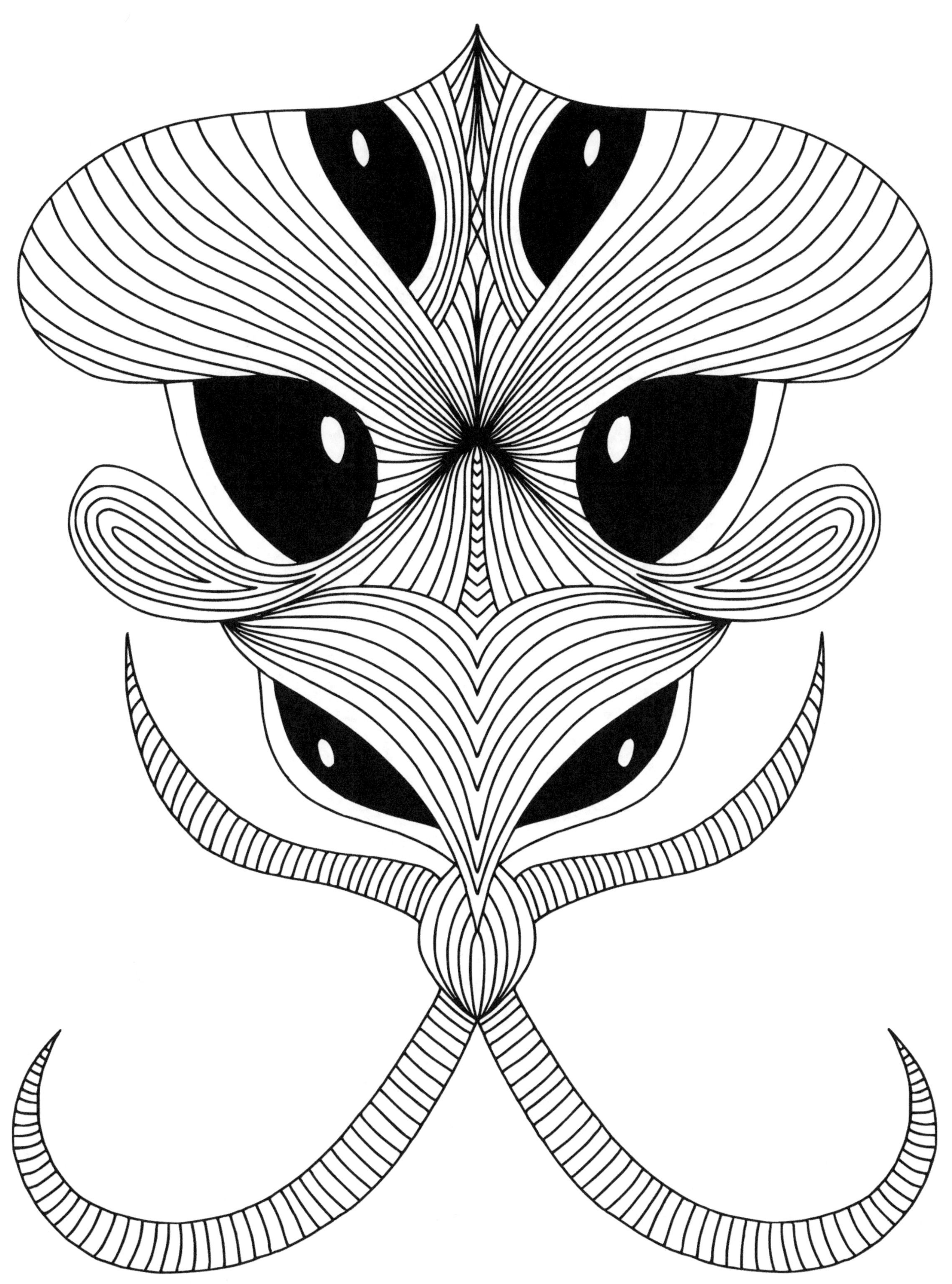

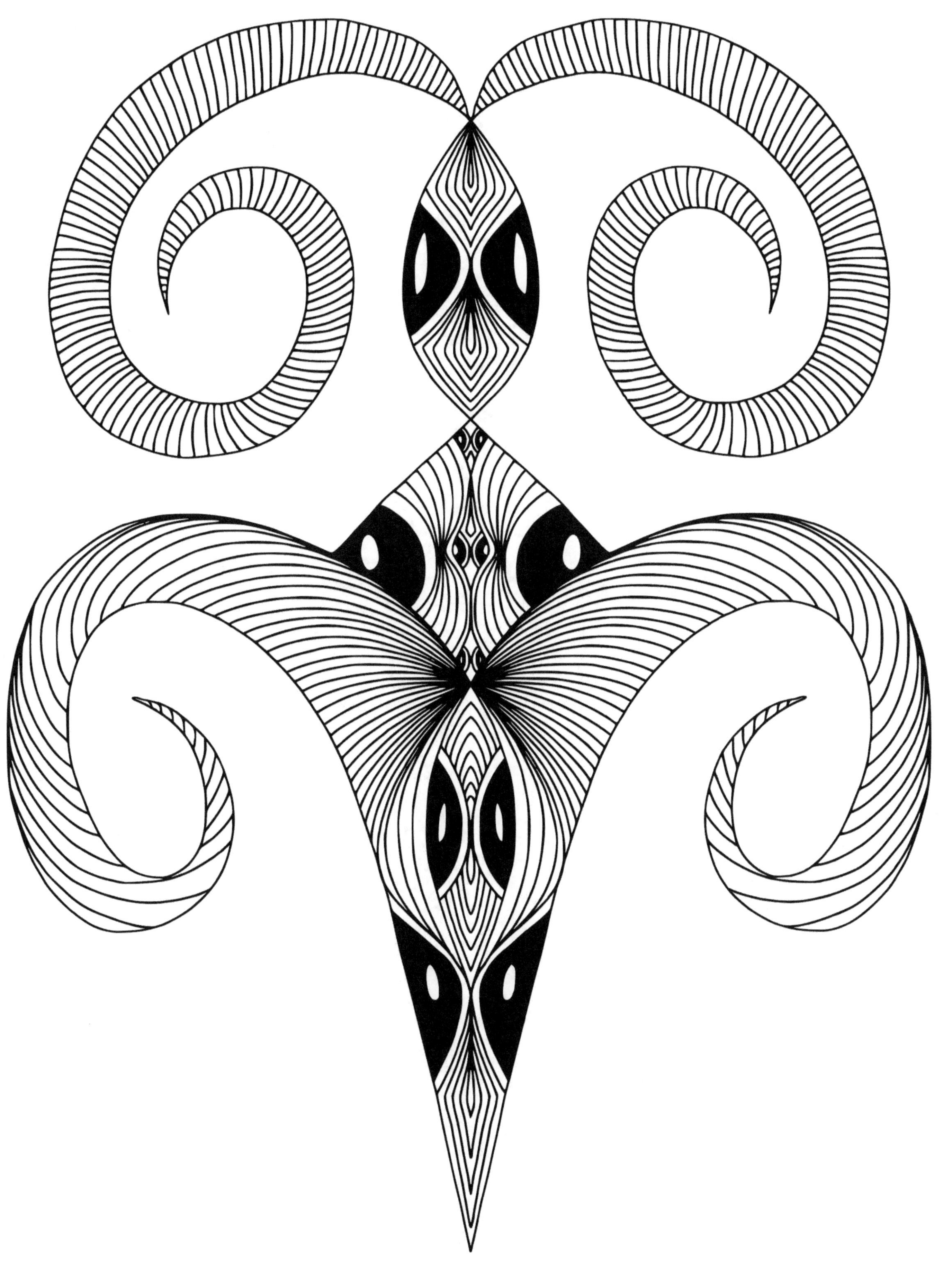

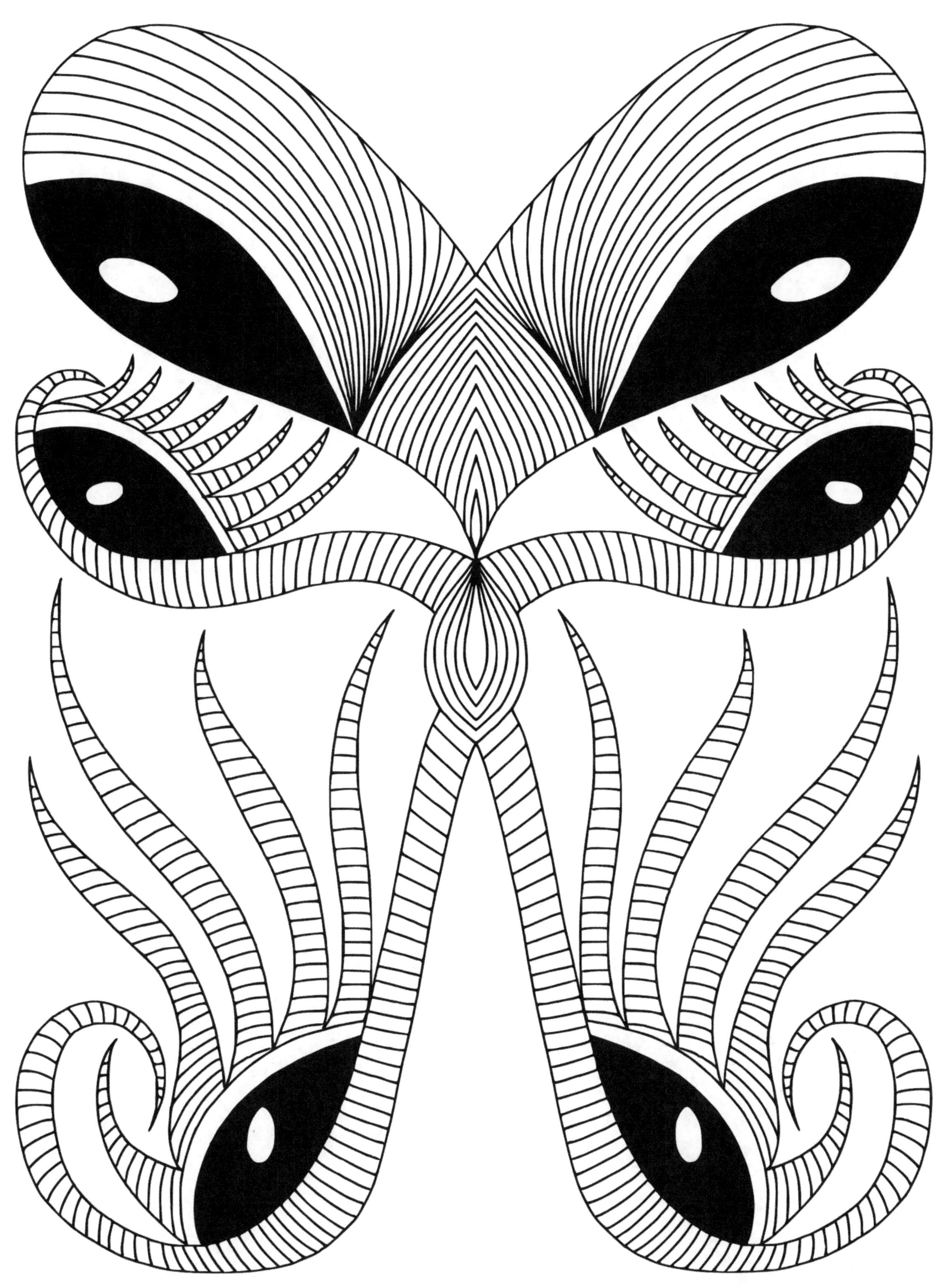

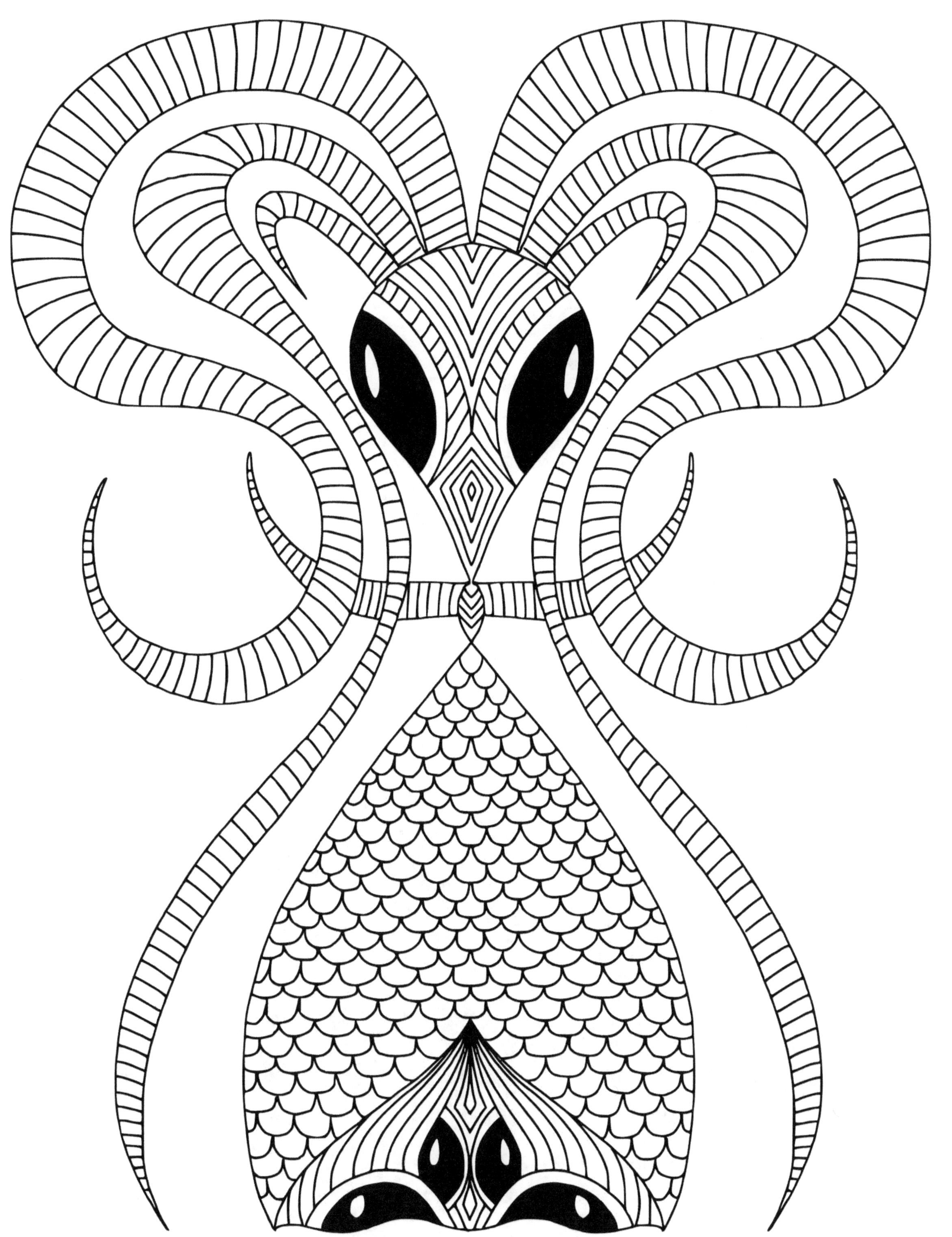

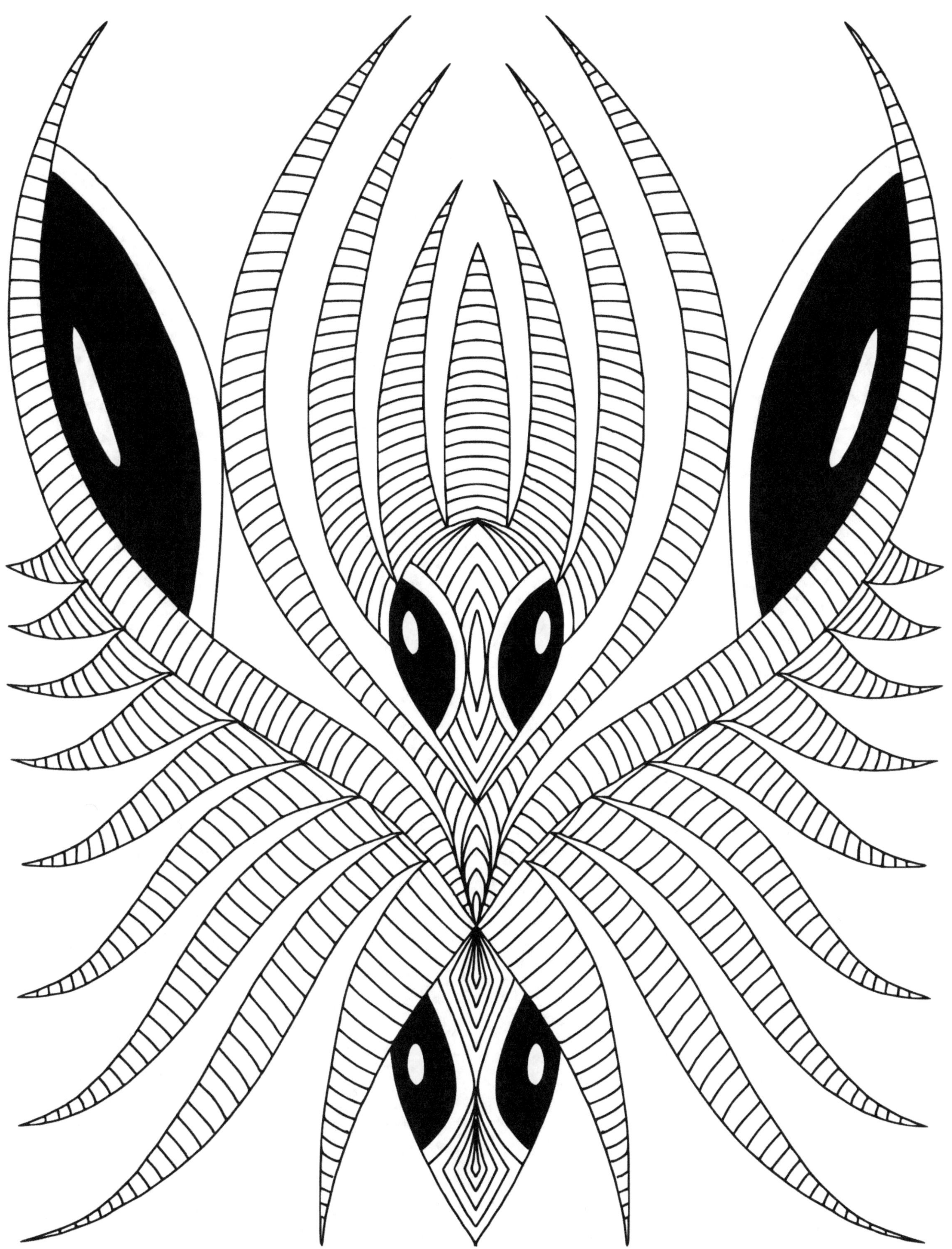

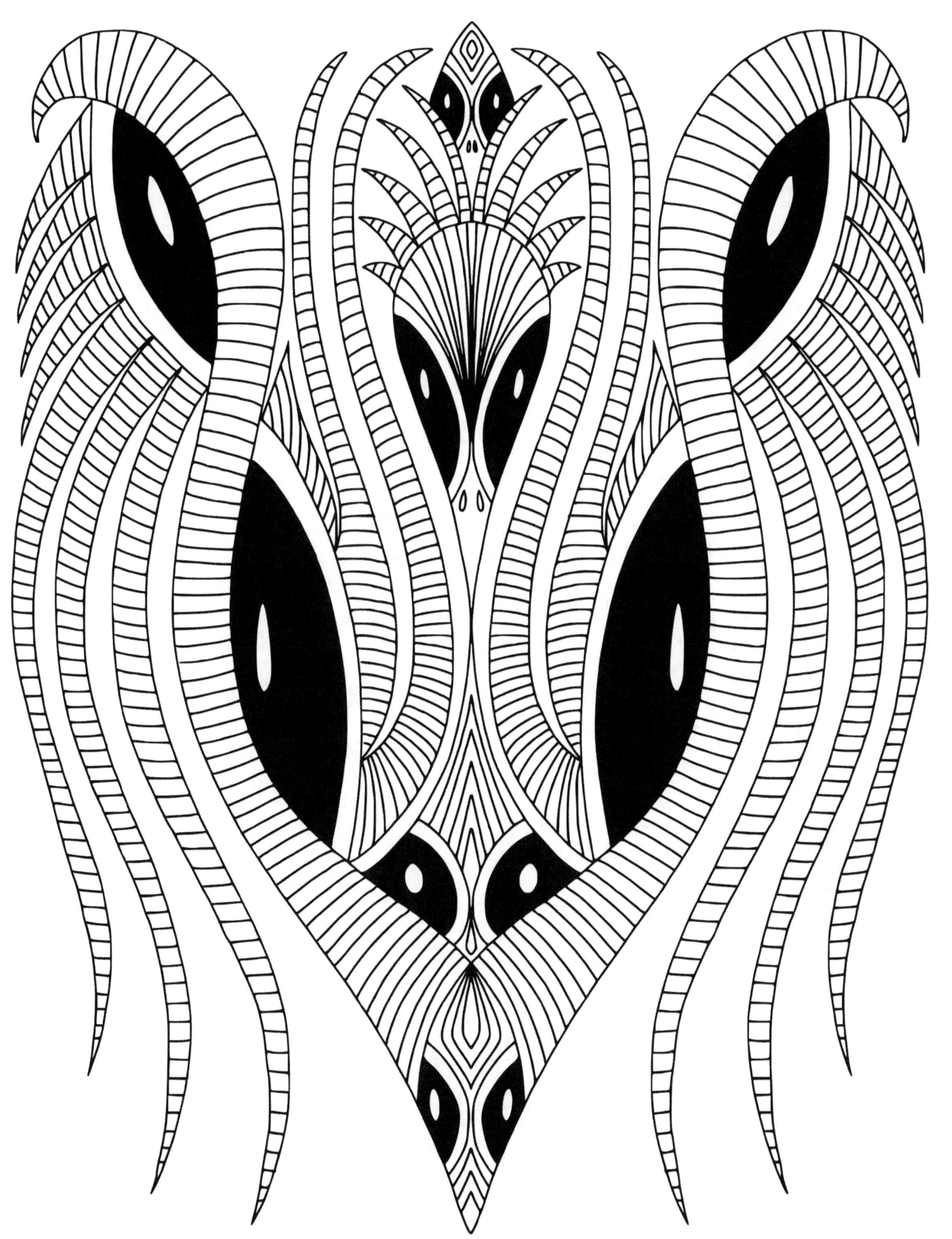

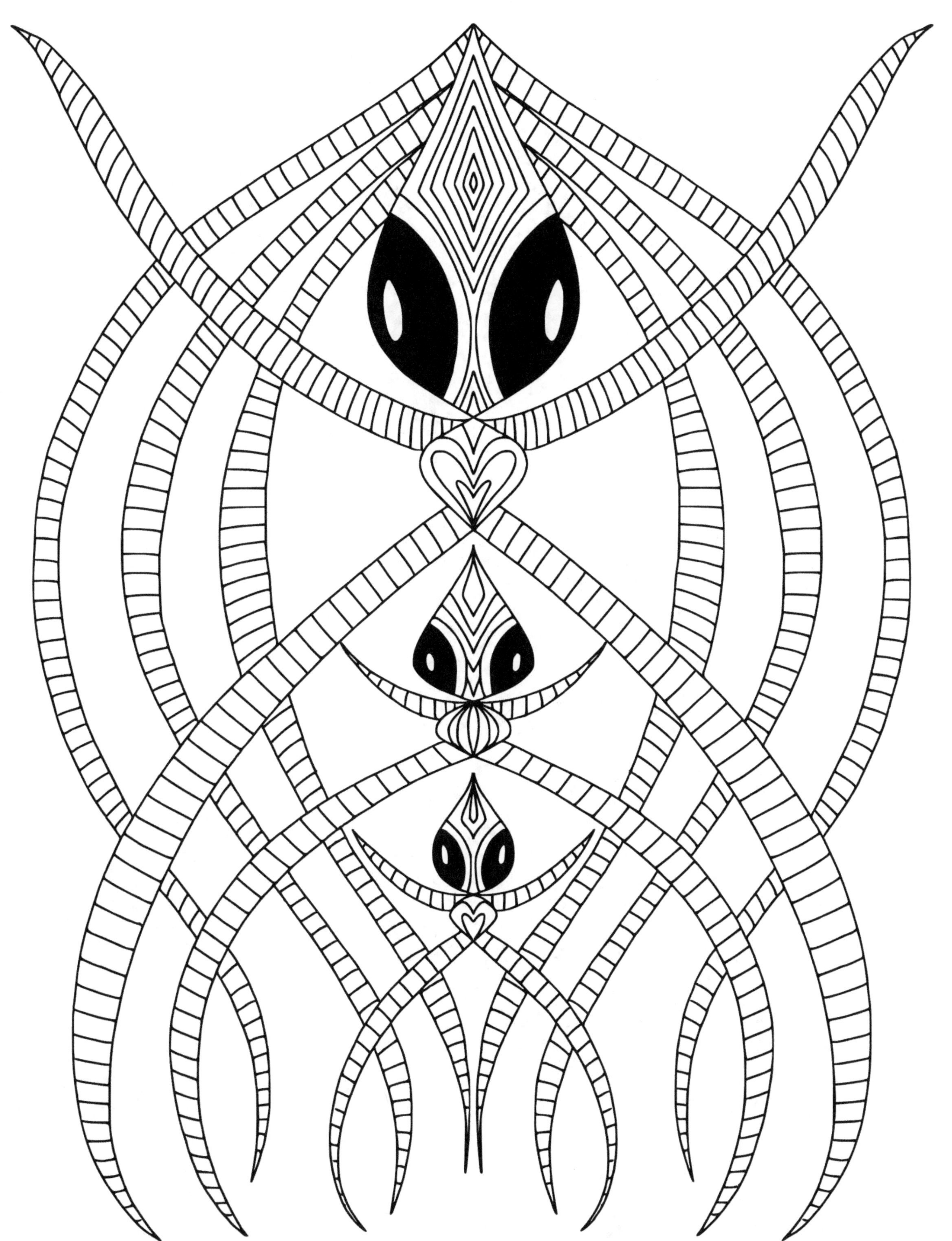

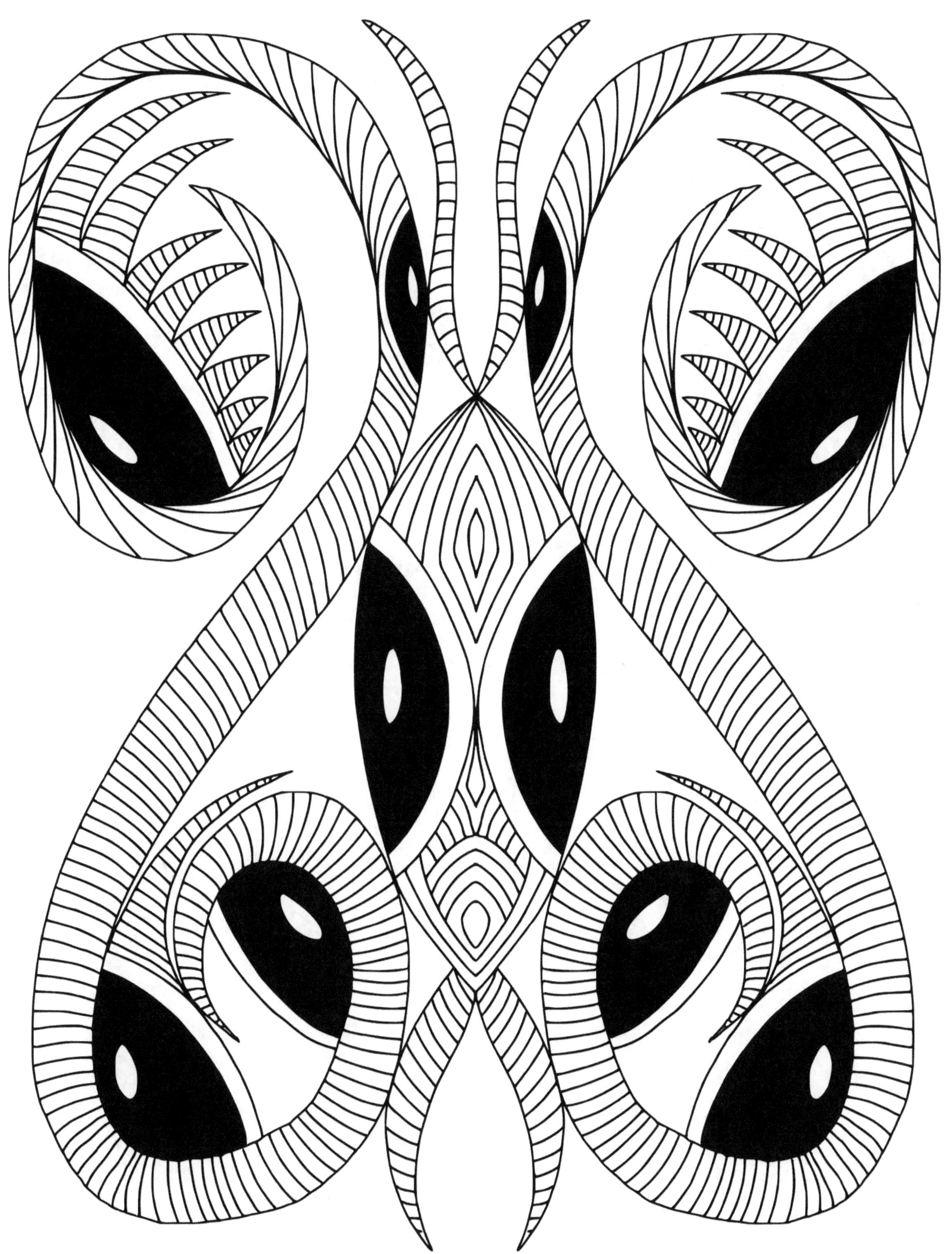

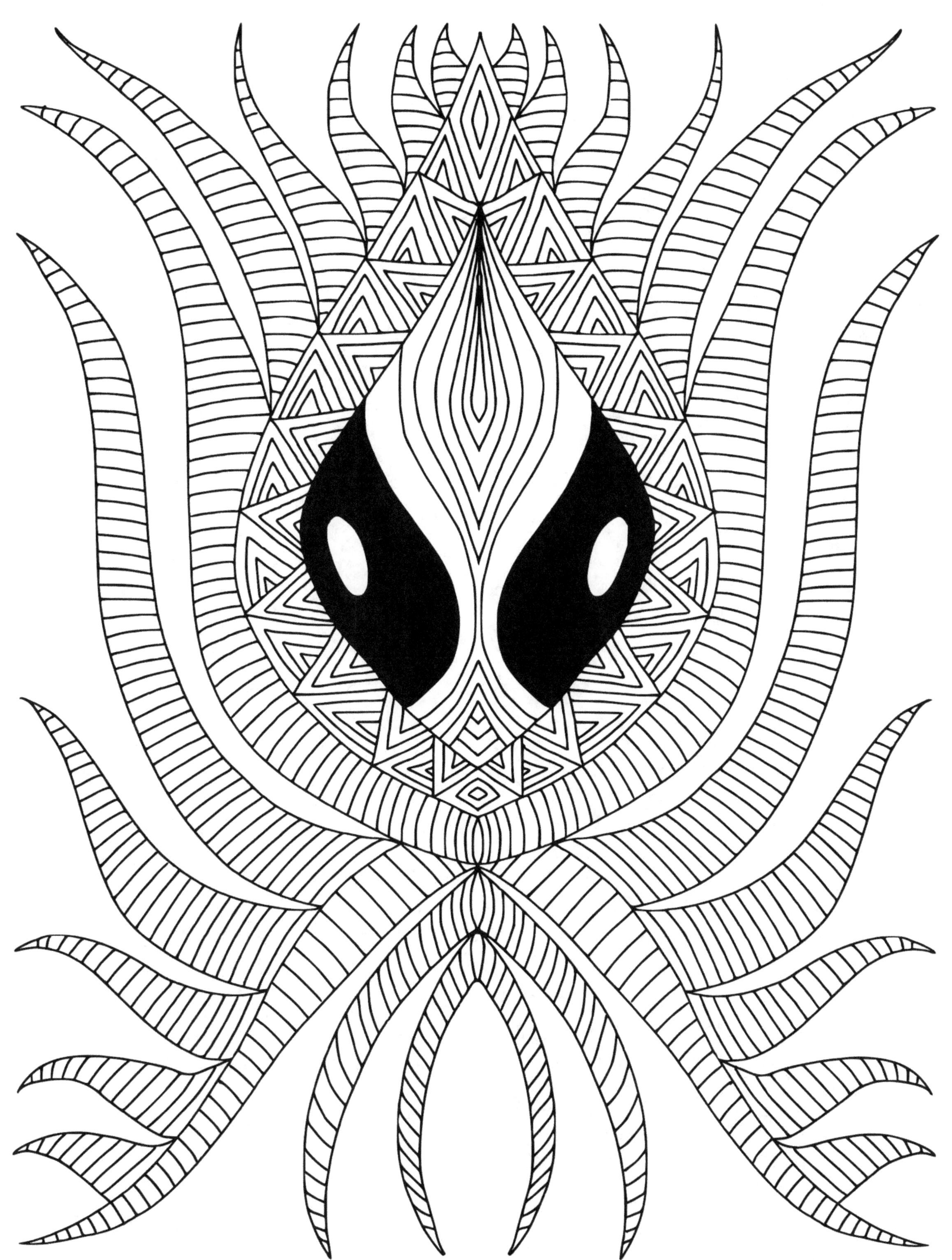

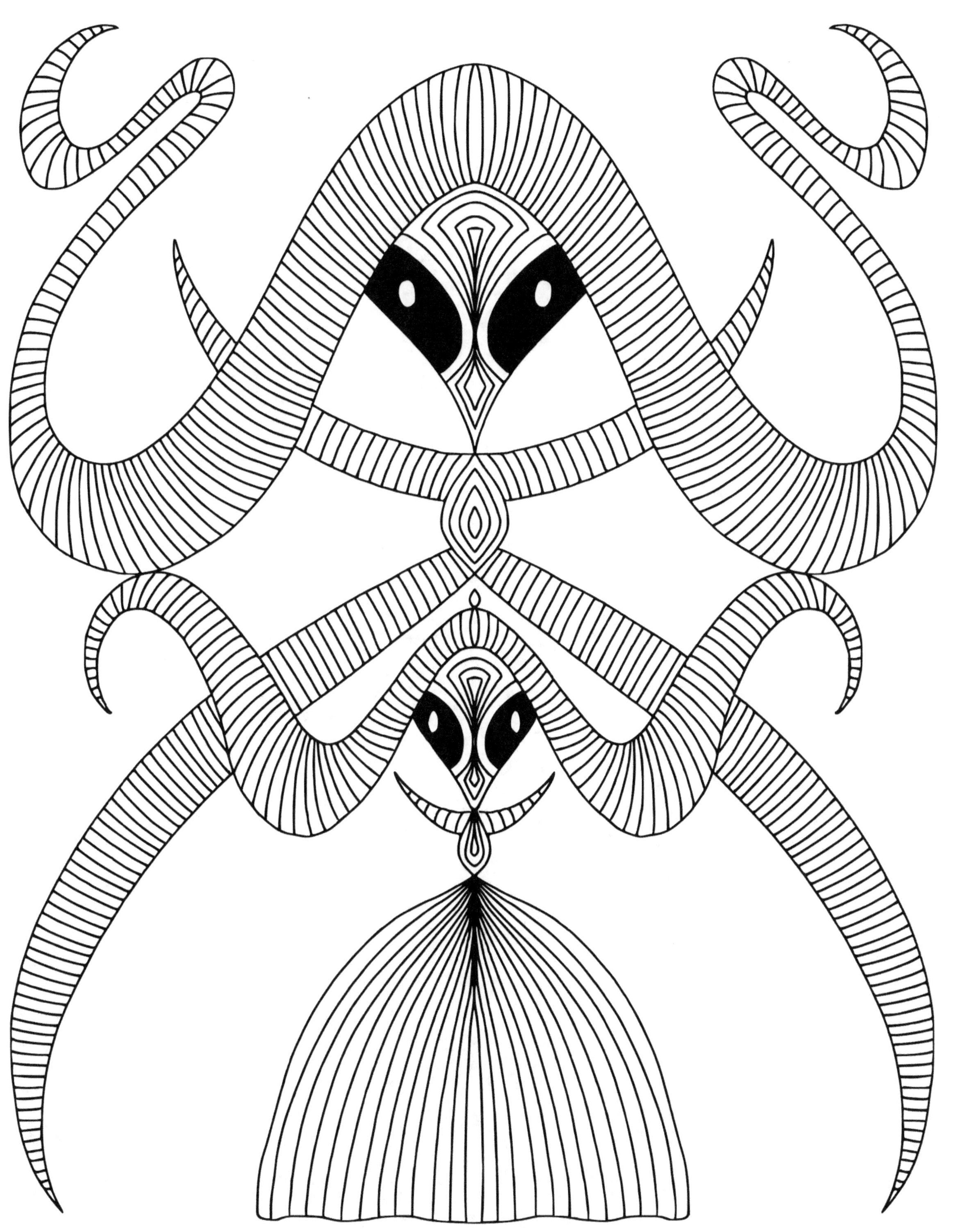

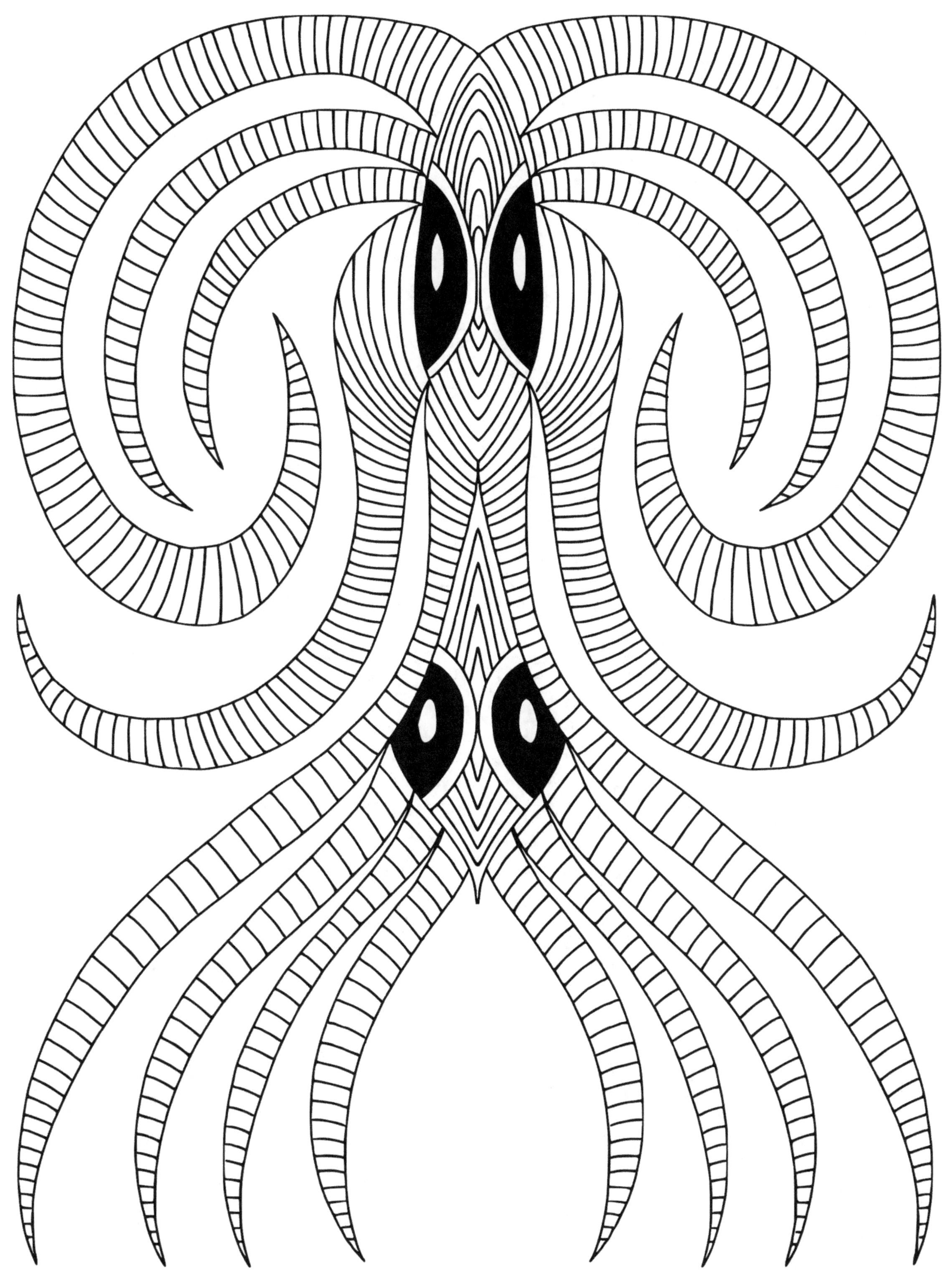

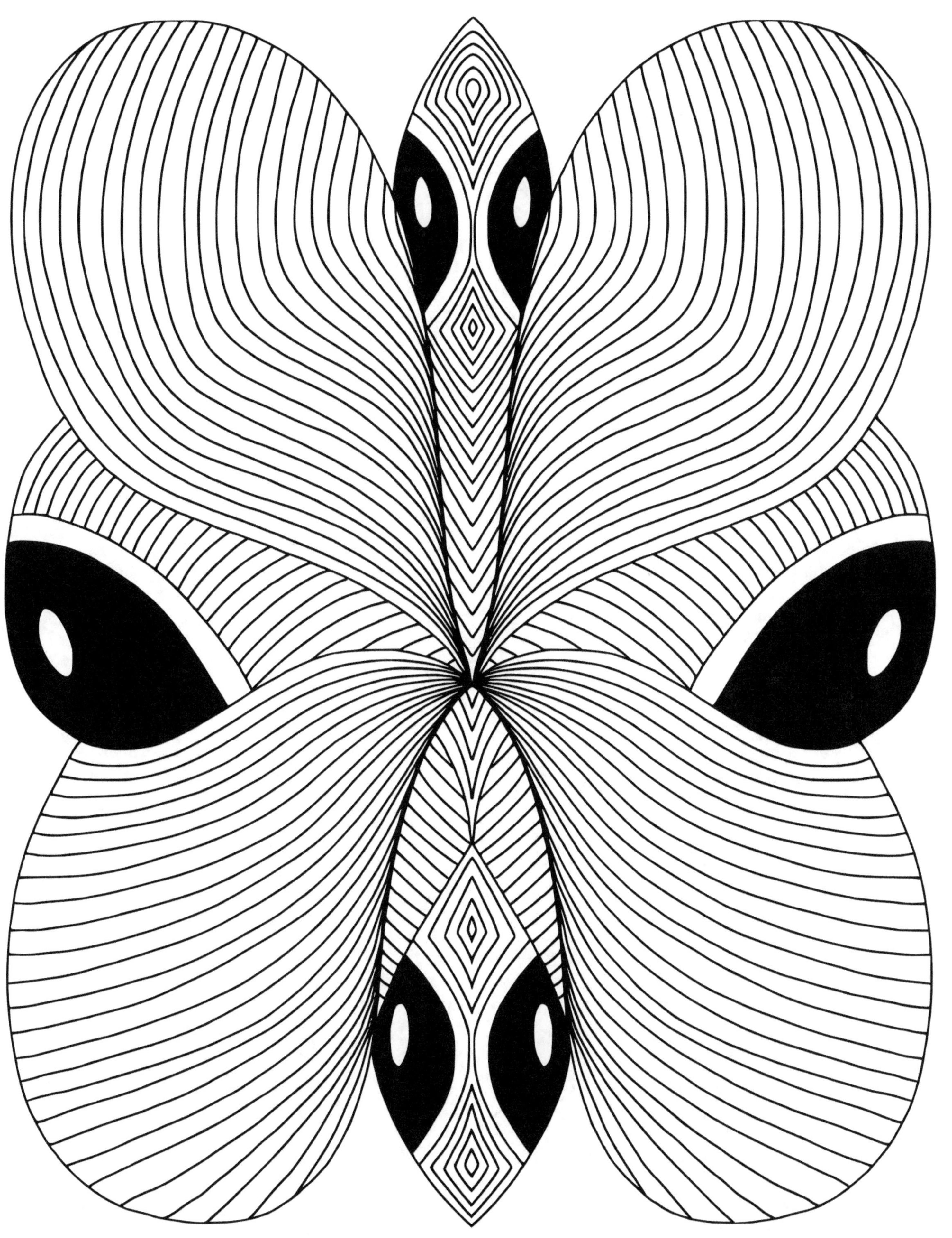

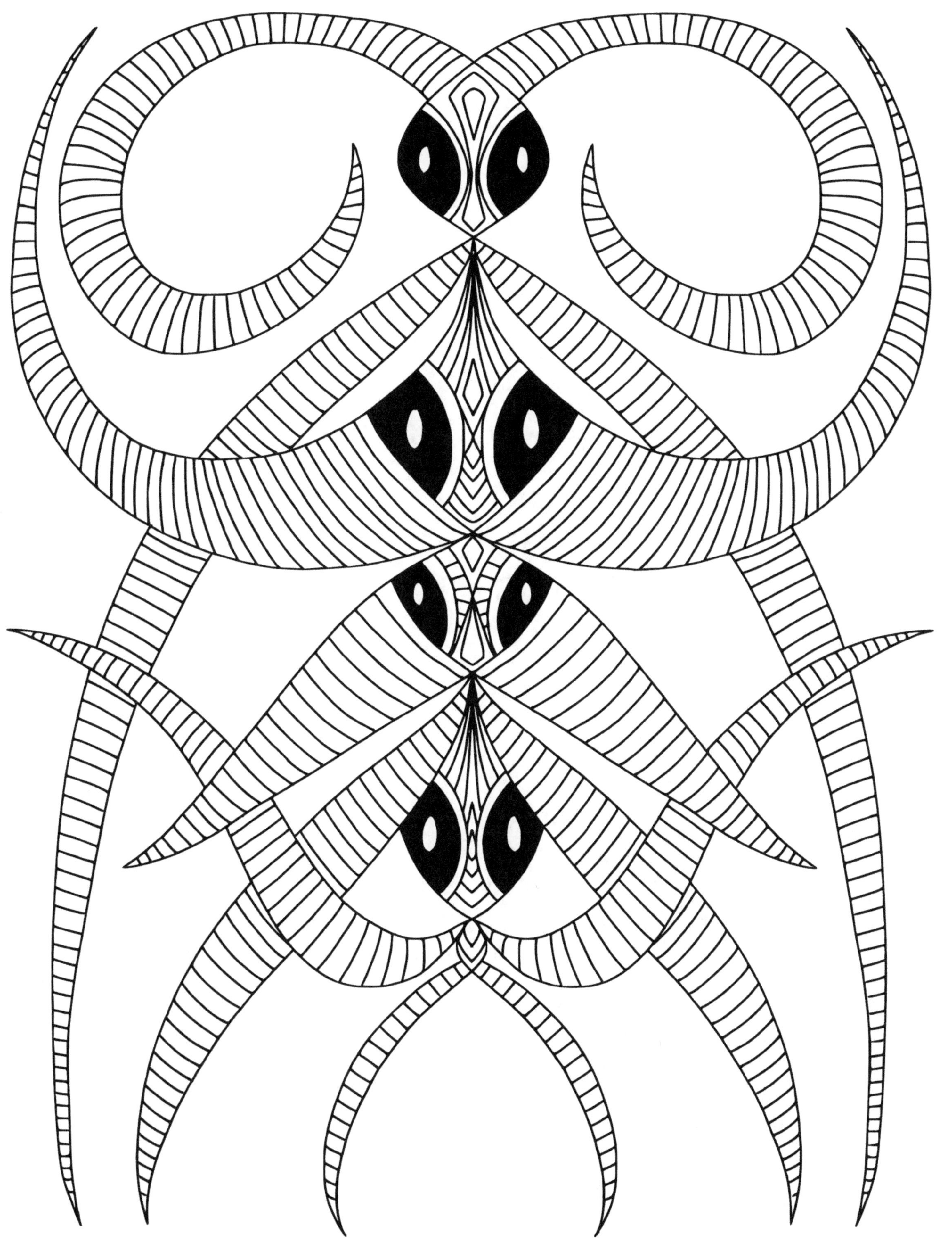

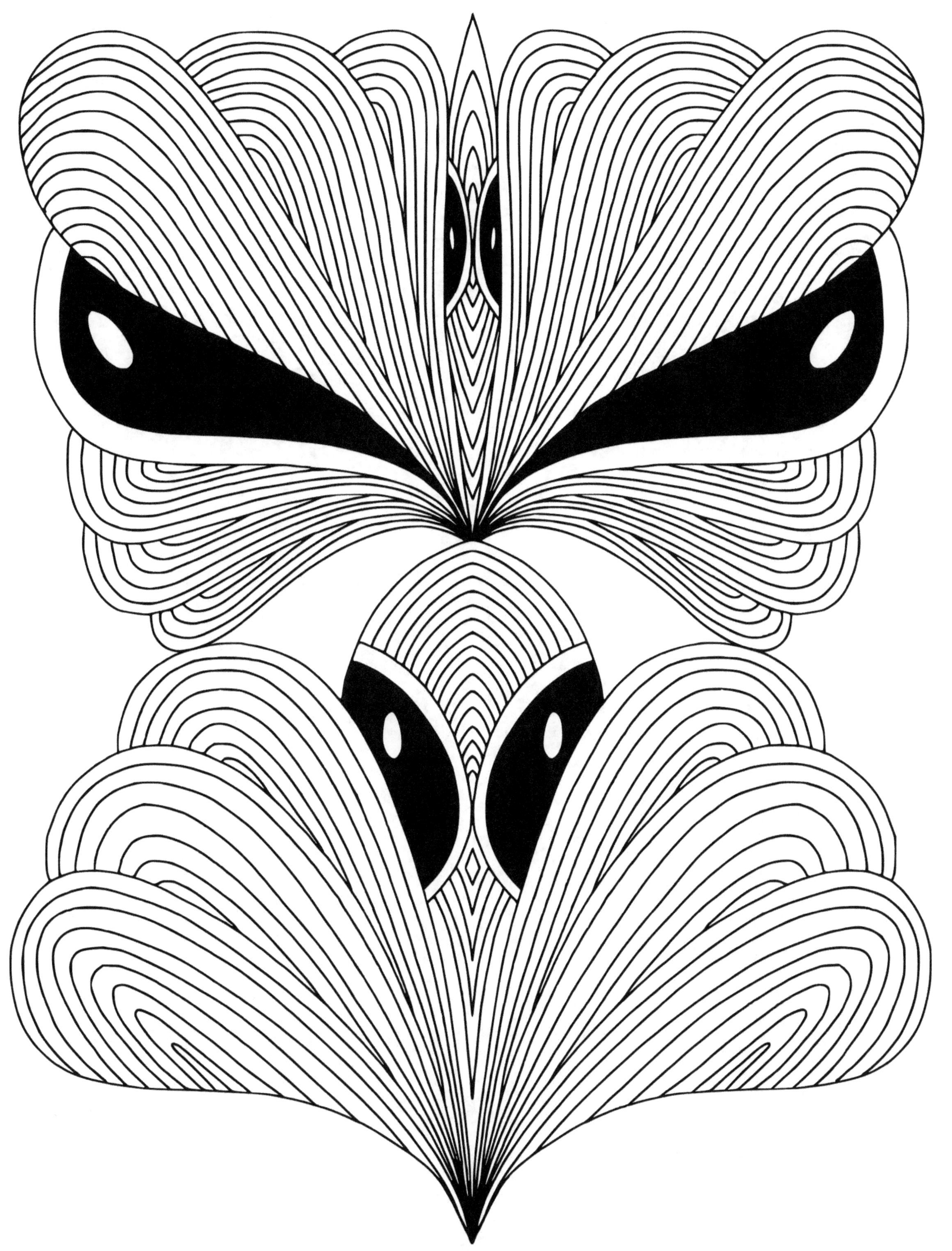

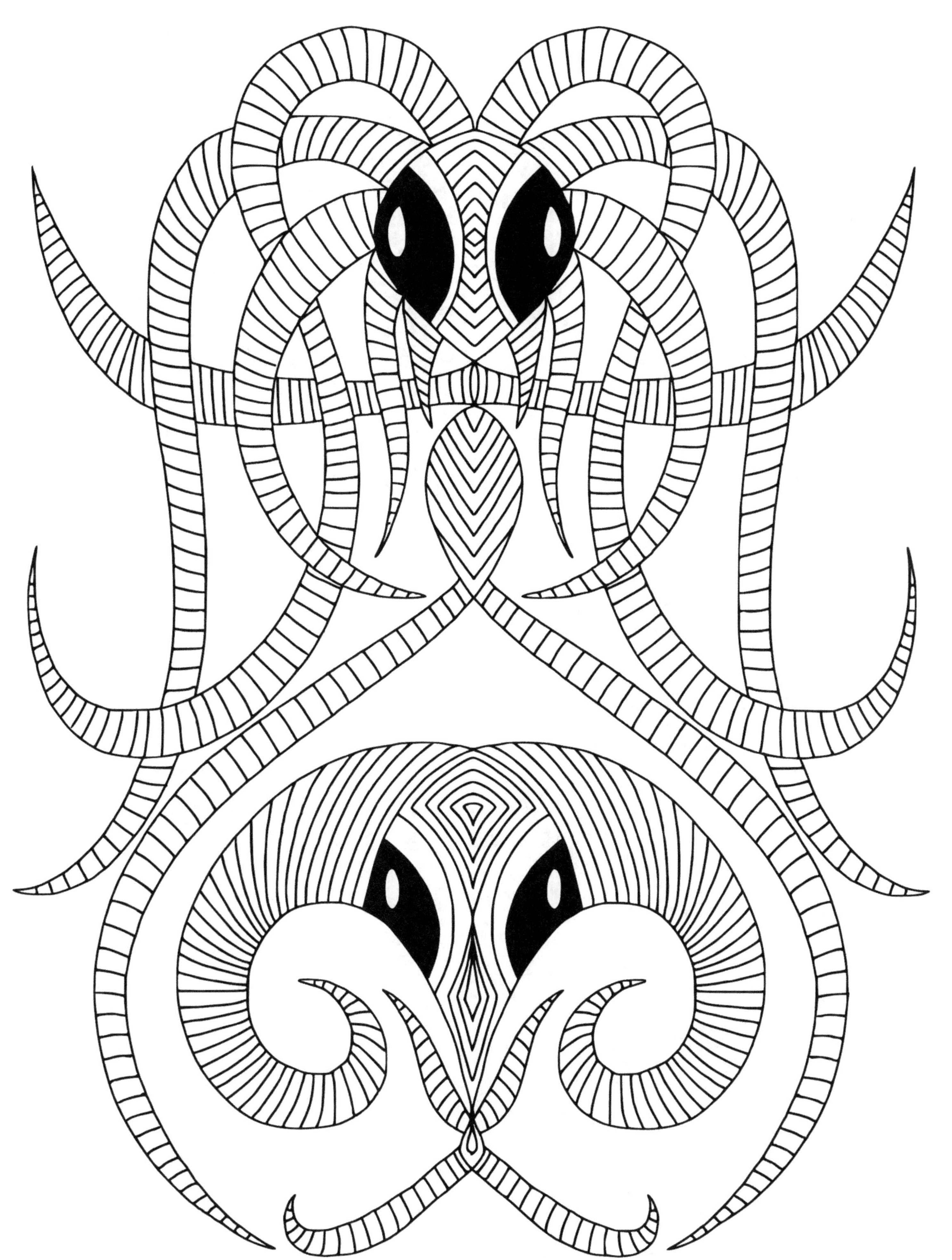

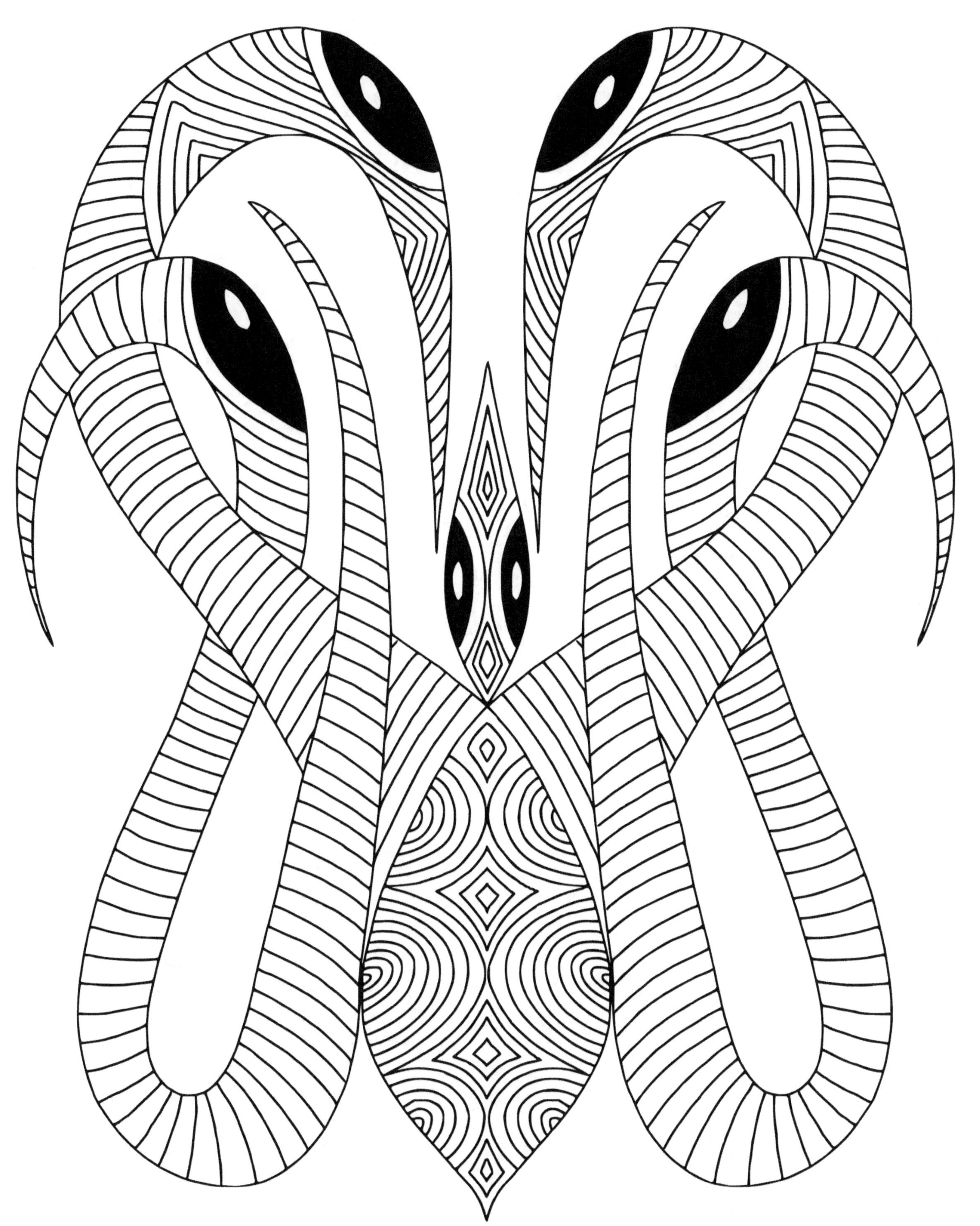

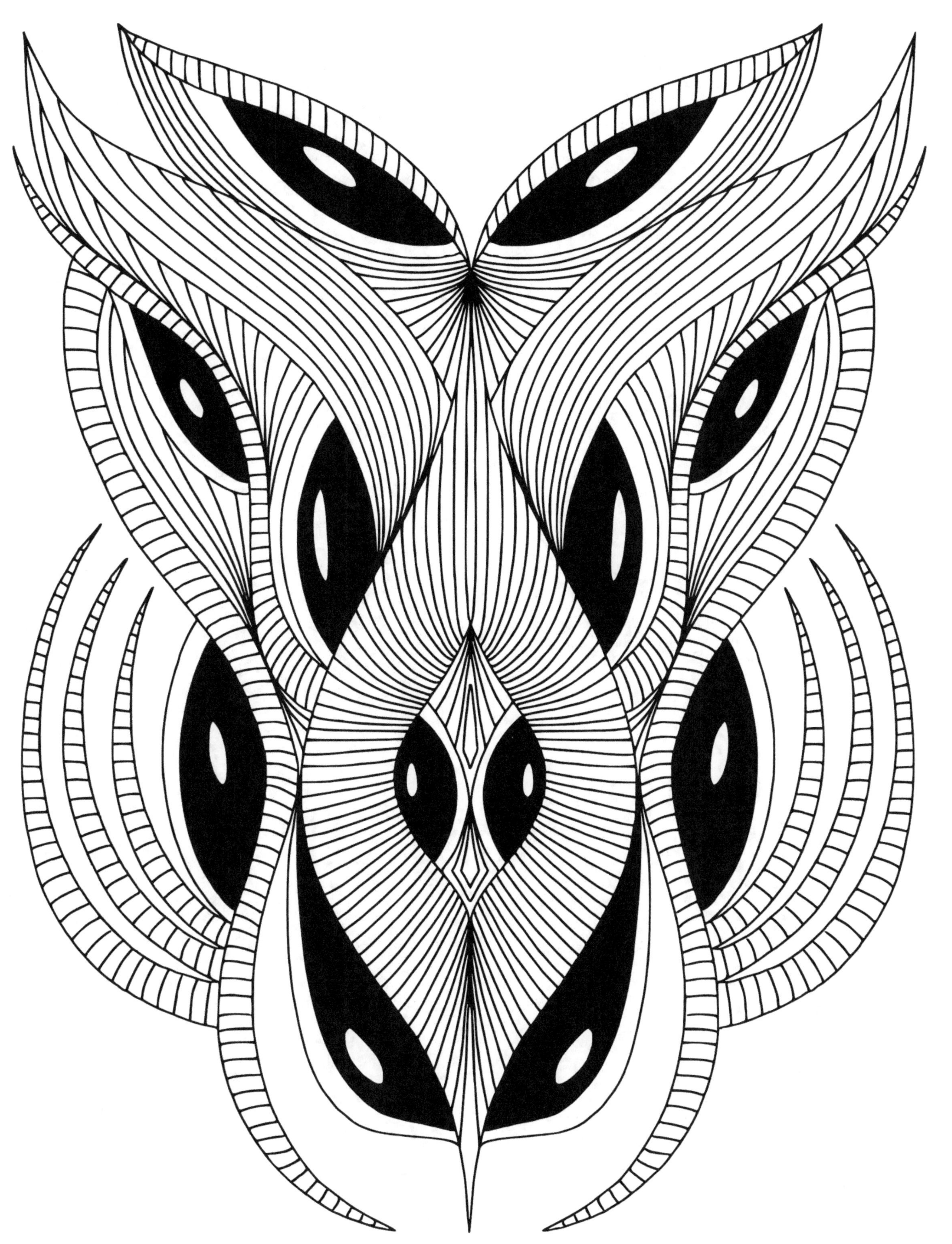

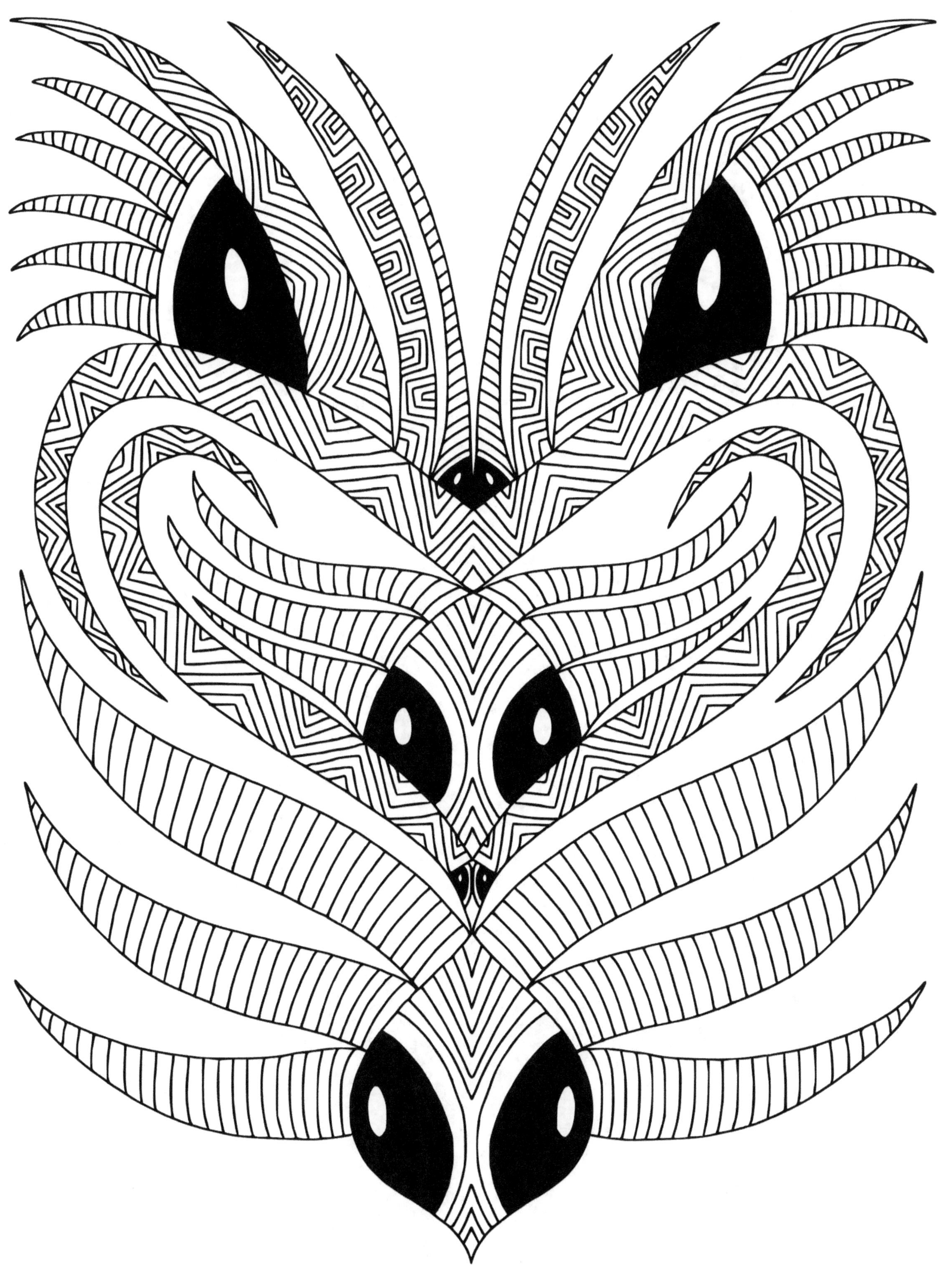

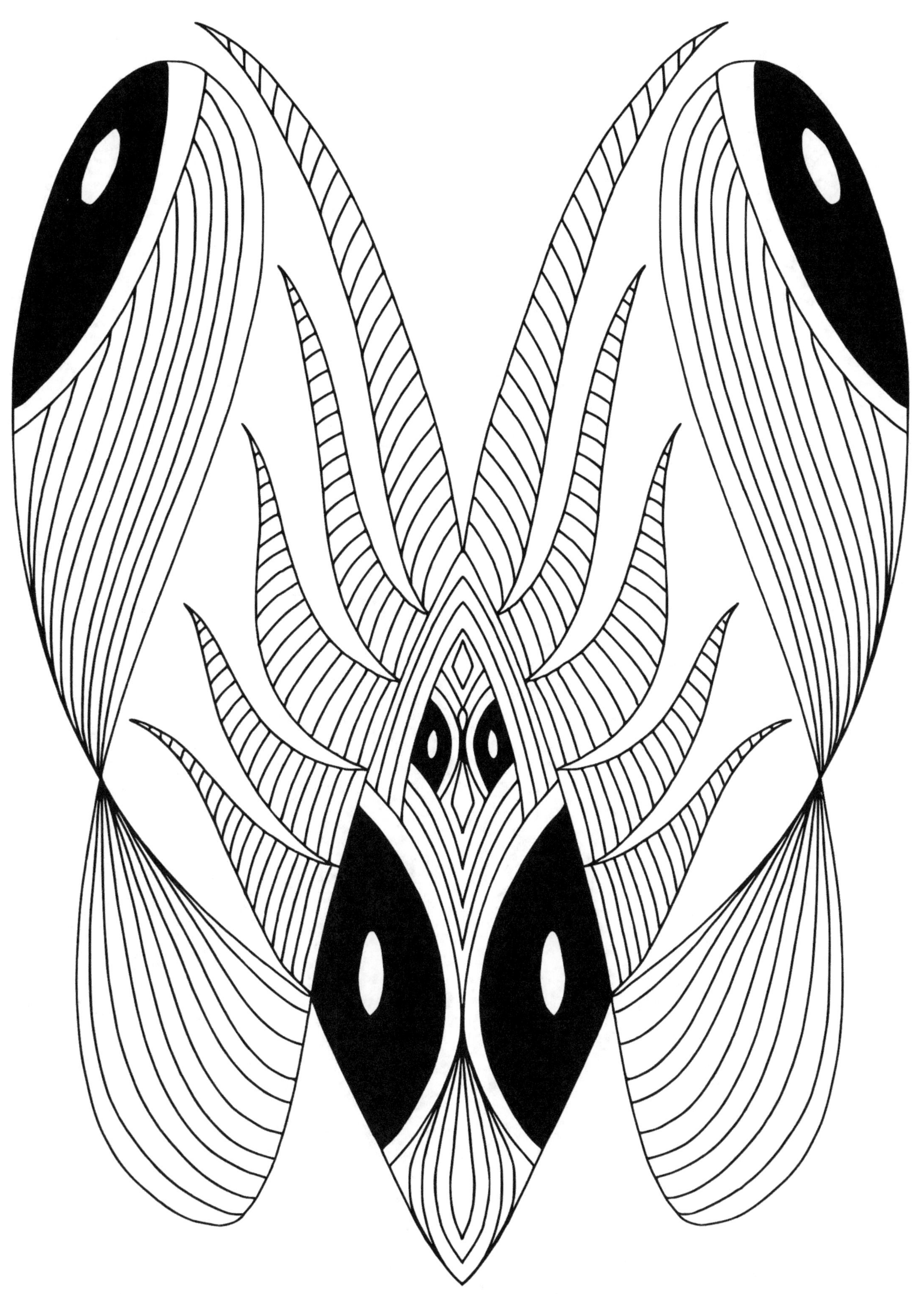

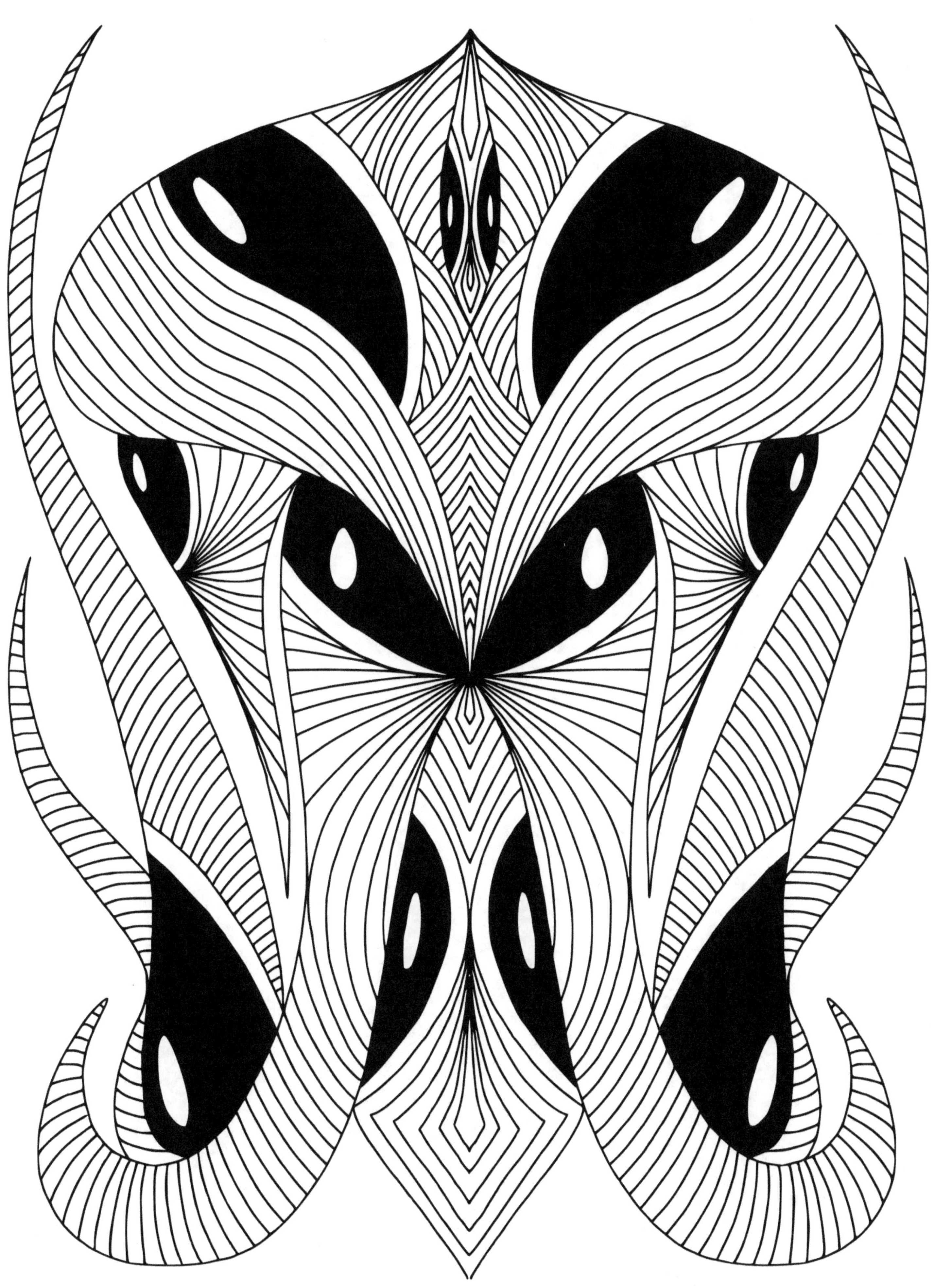

Bonus   Upside Down versions.......

Bonus   Upside Down versions.......

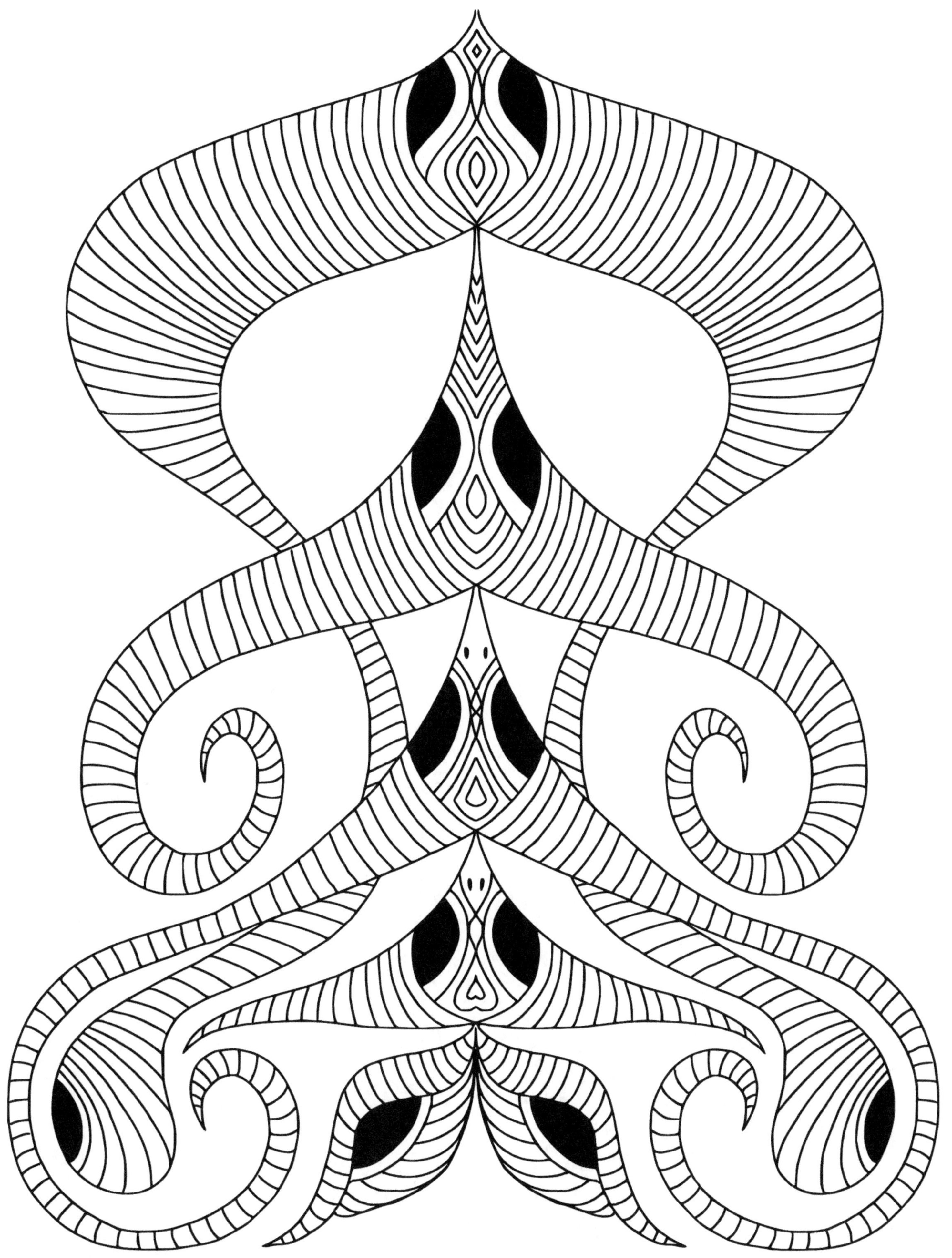

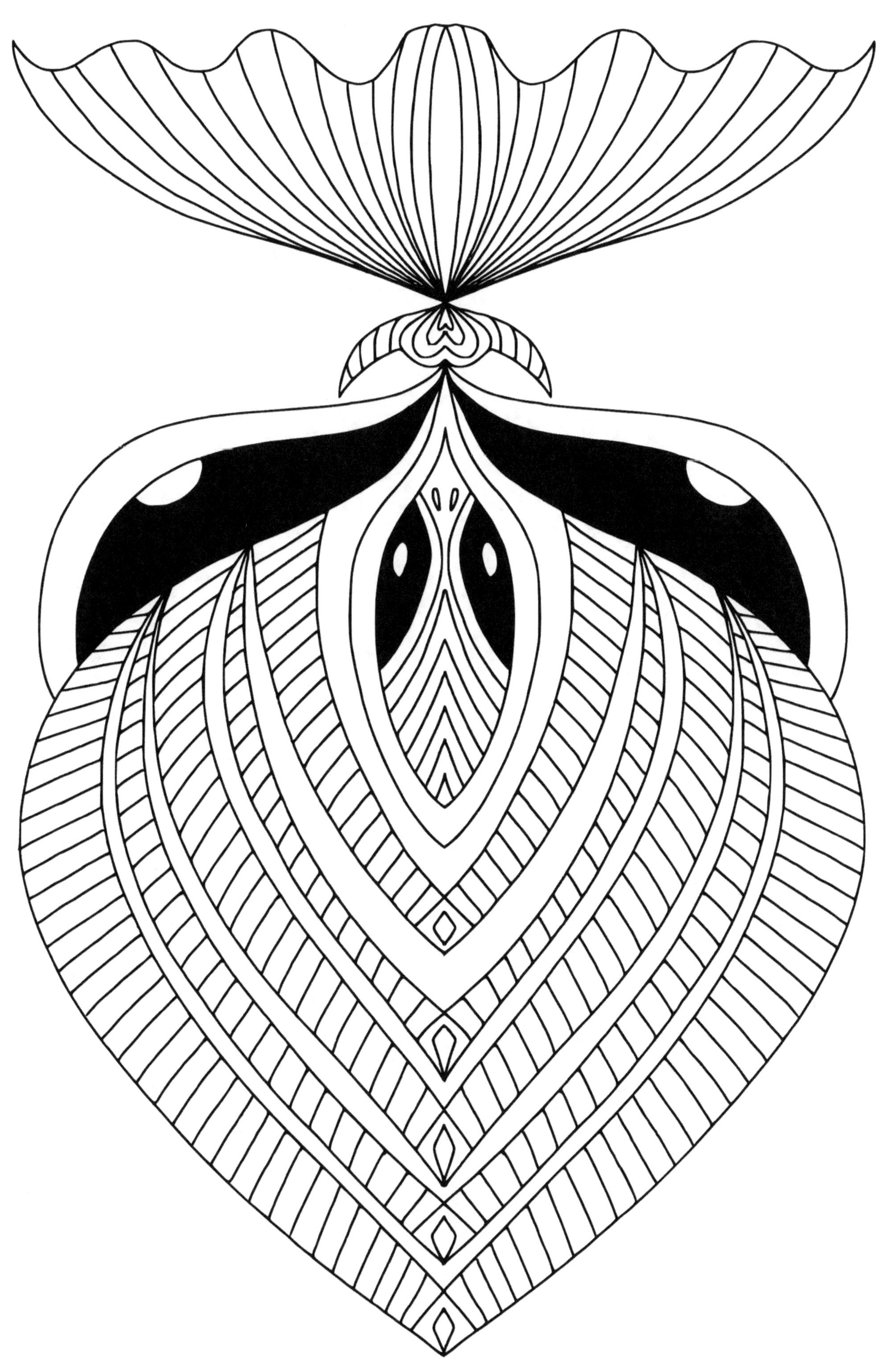

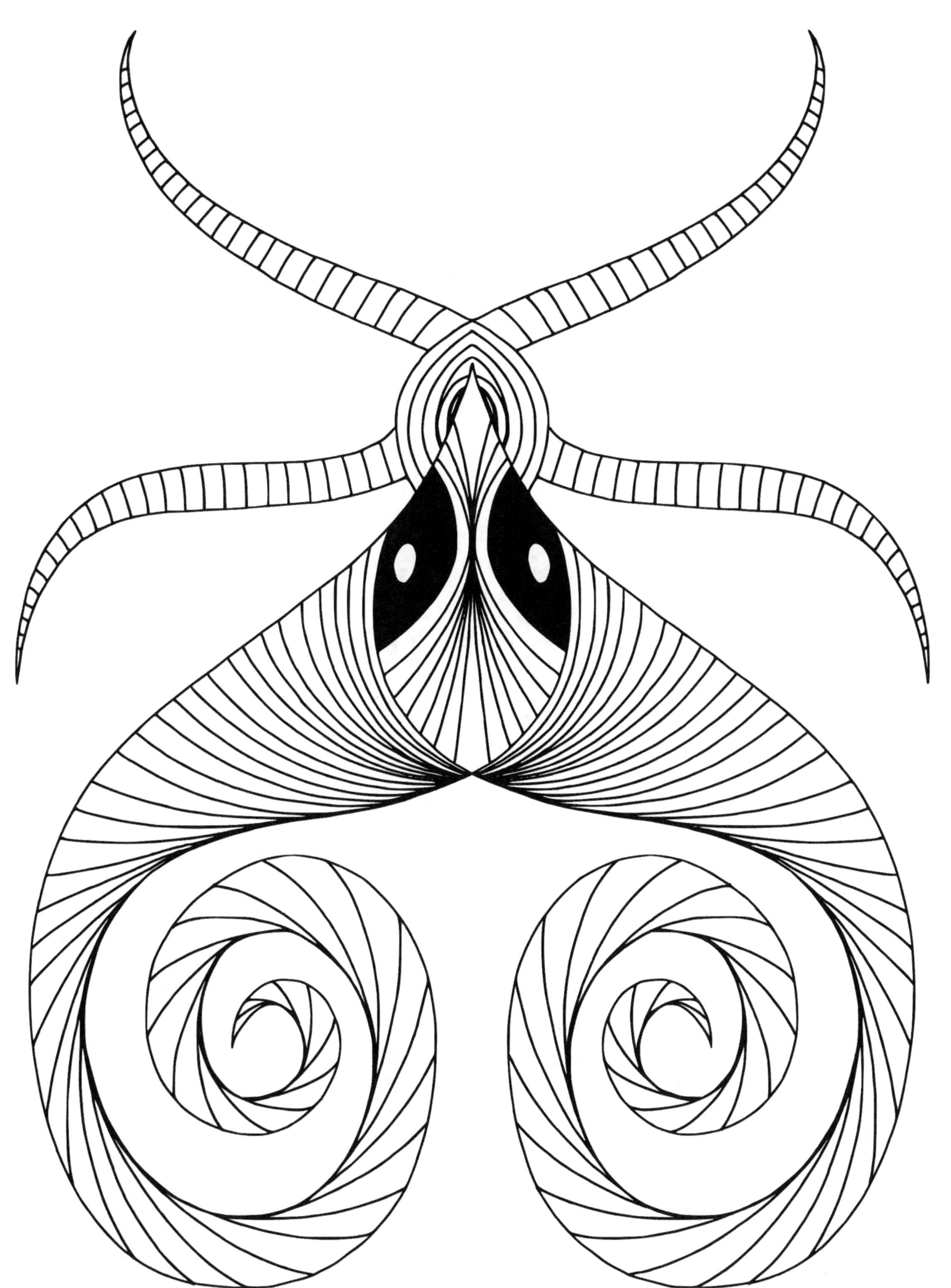

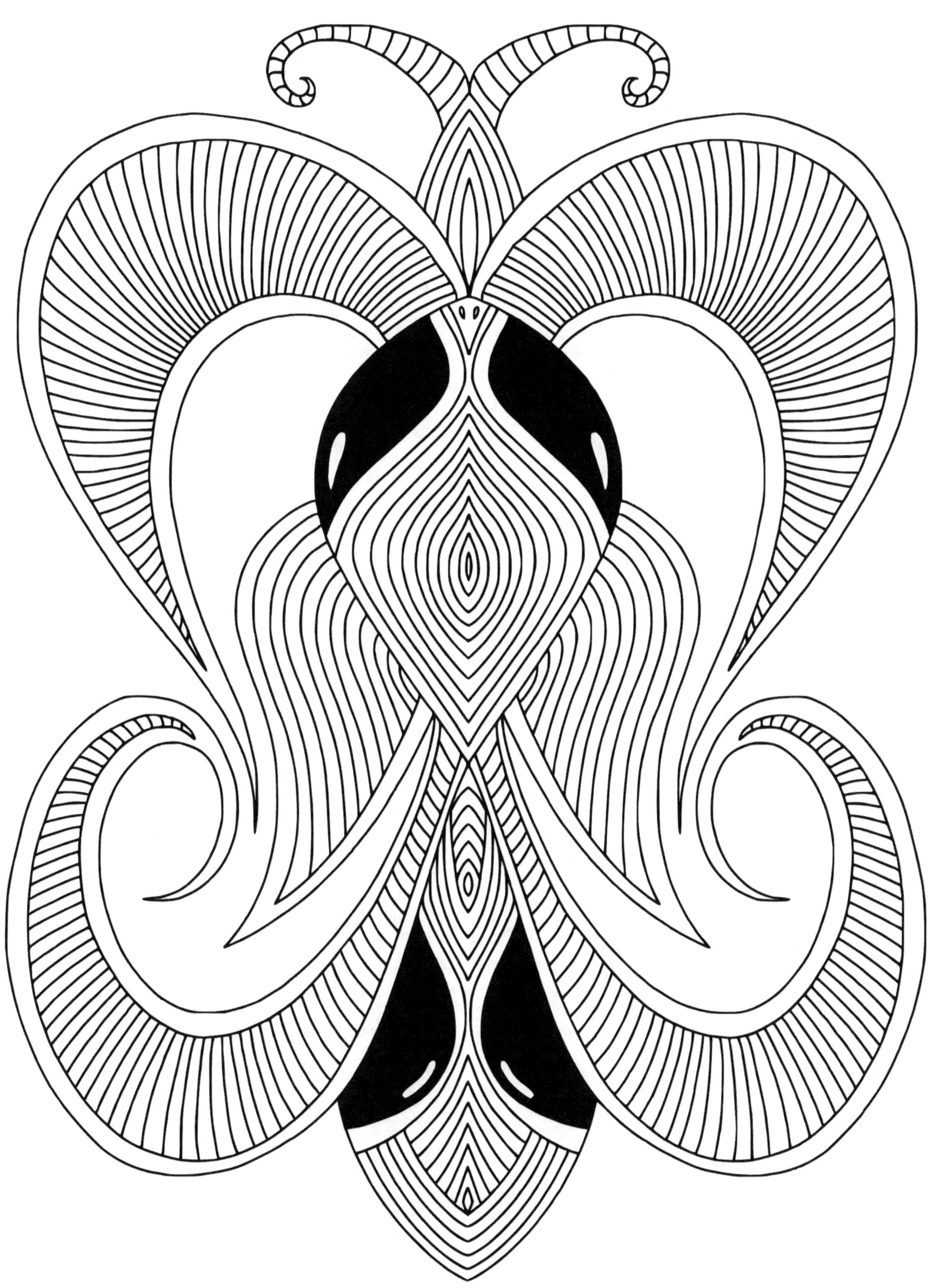

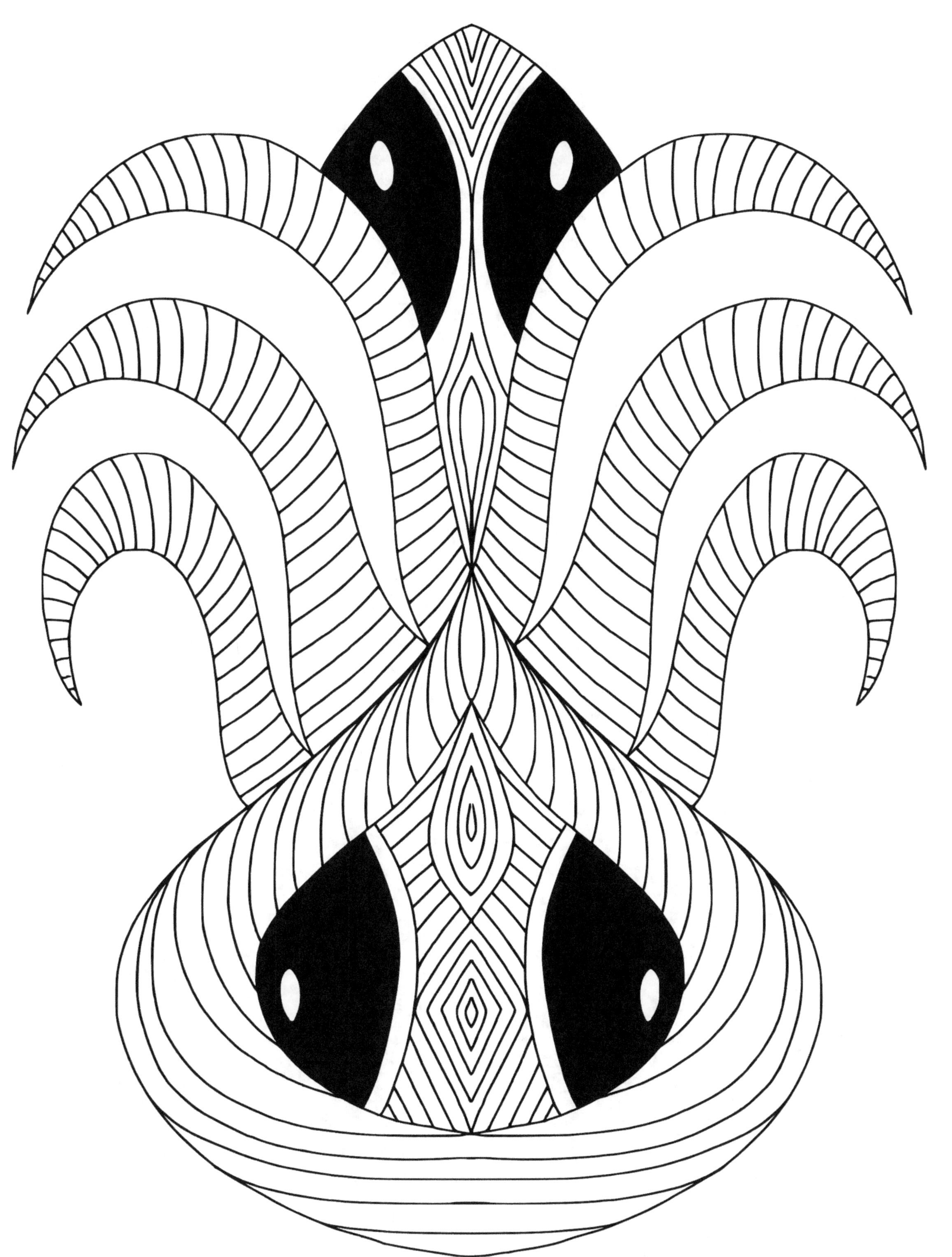

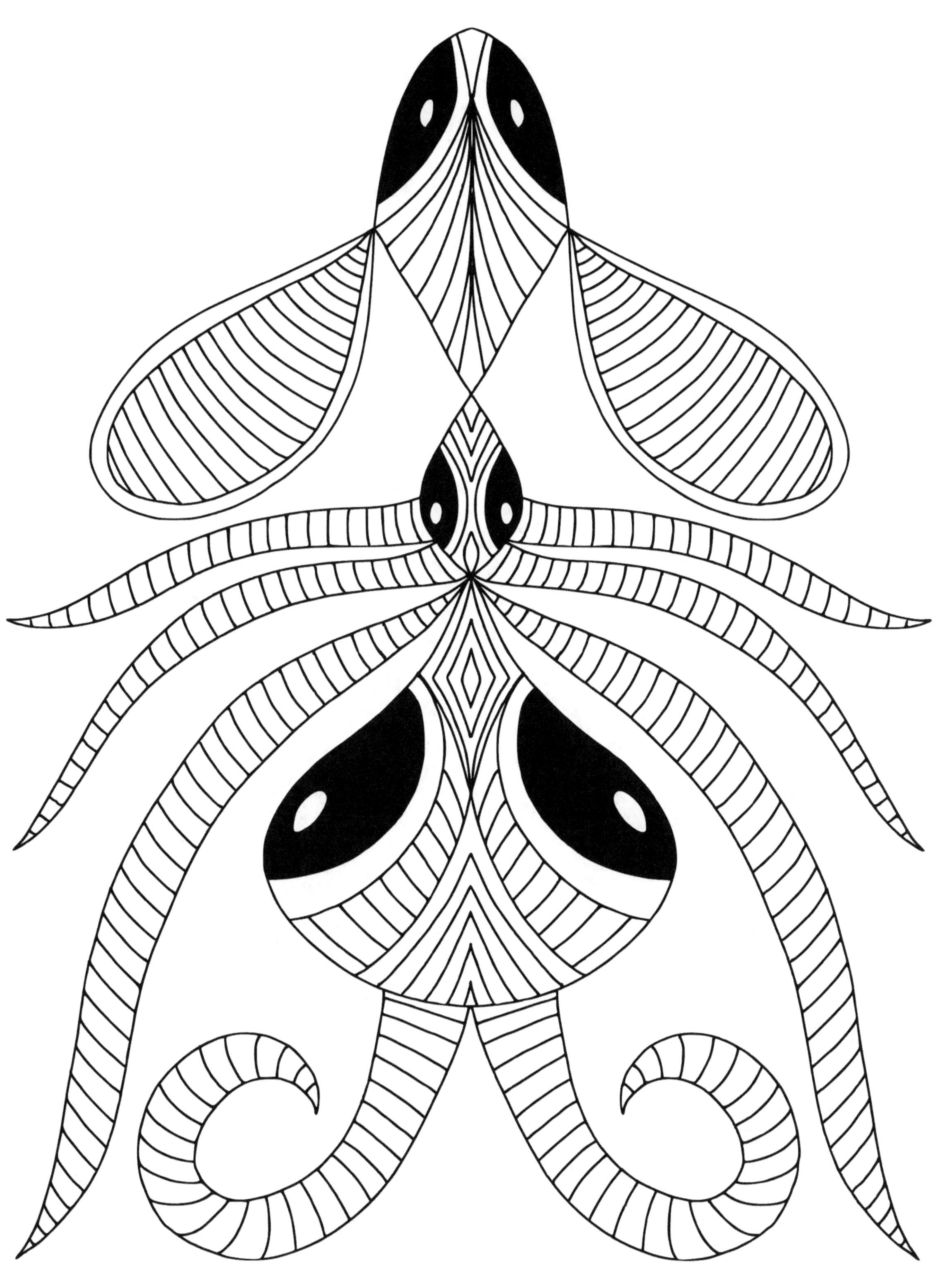

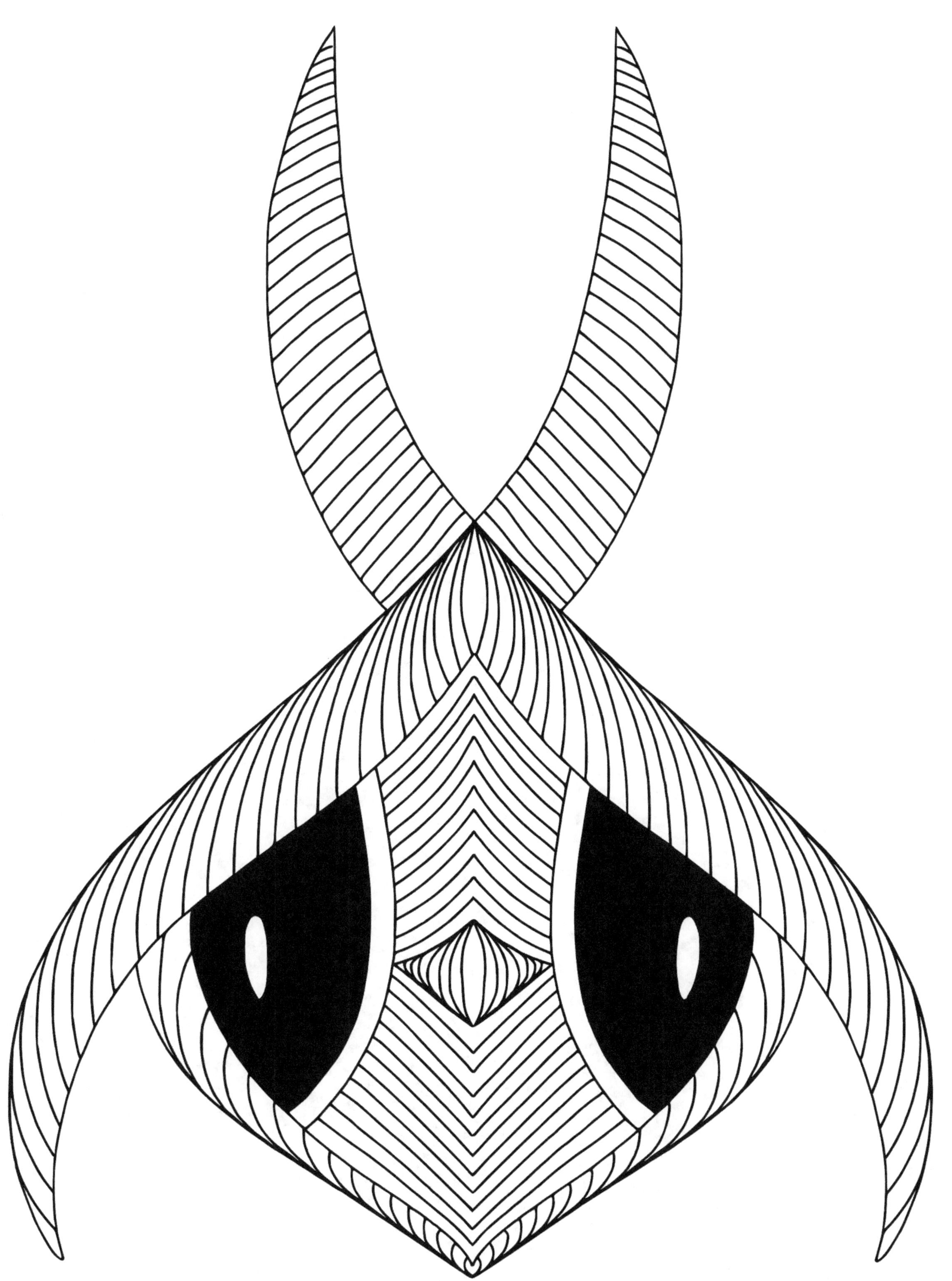

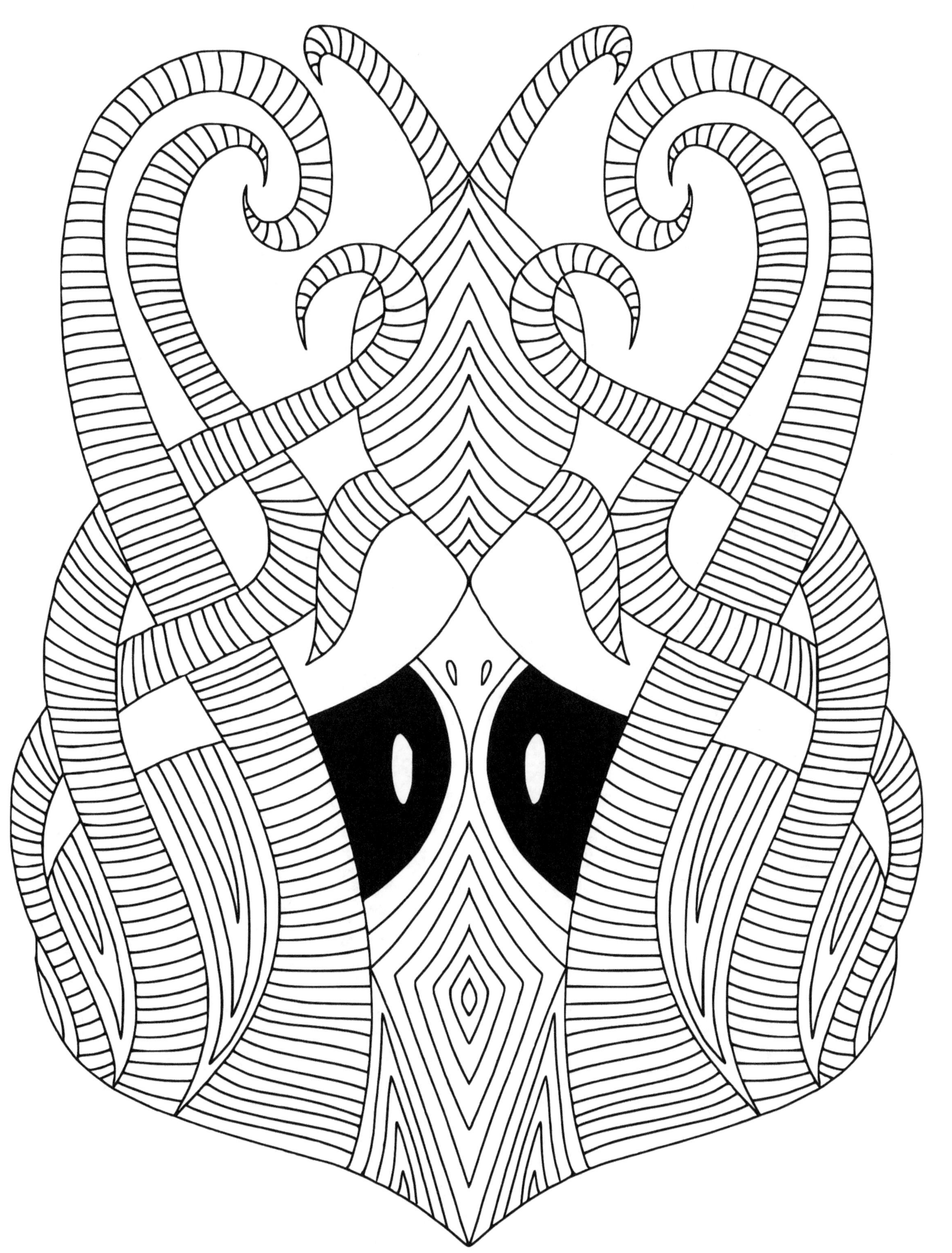

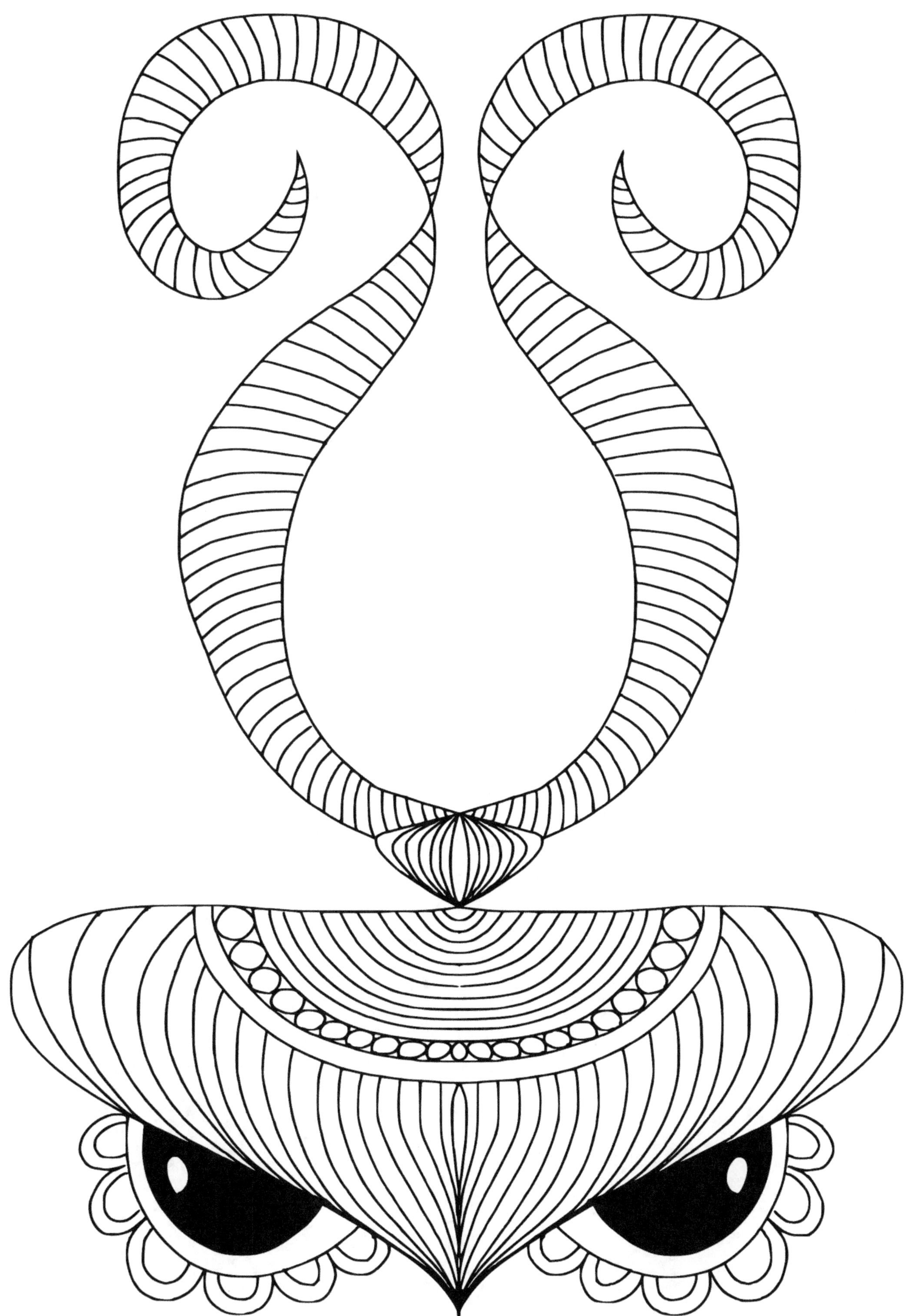

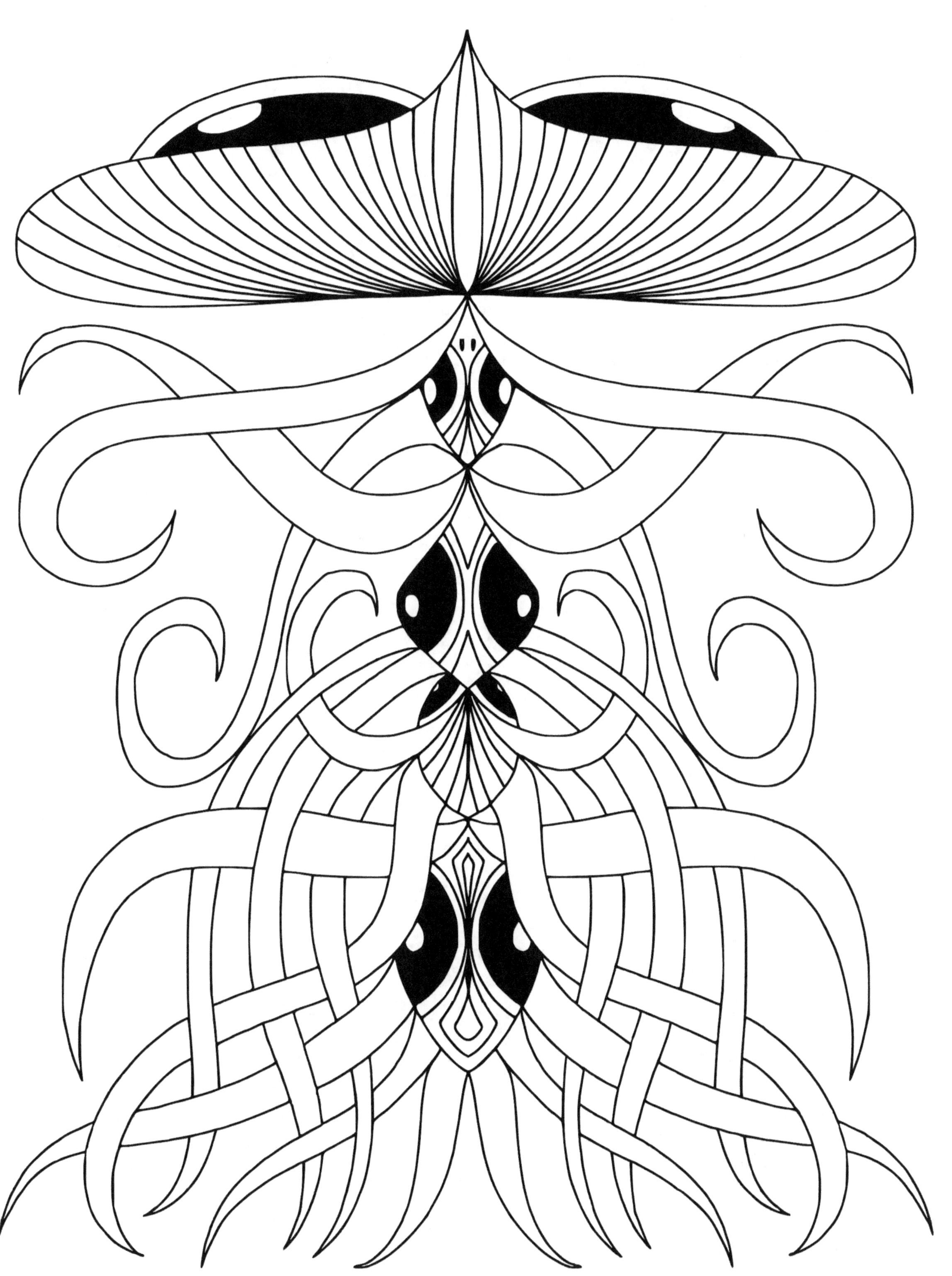

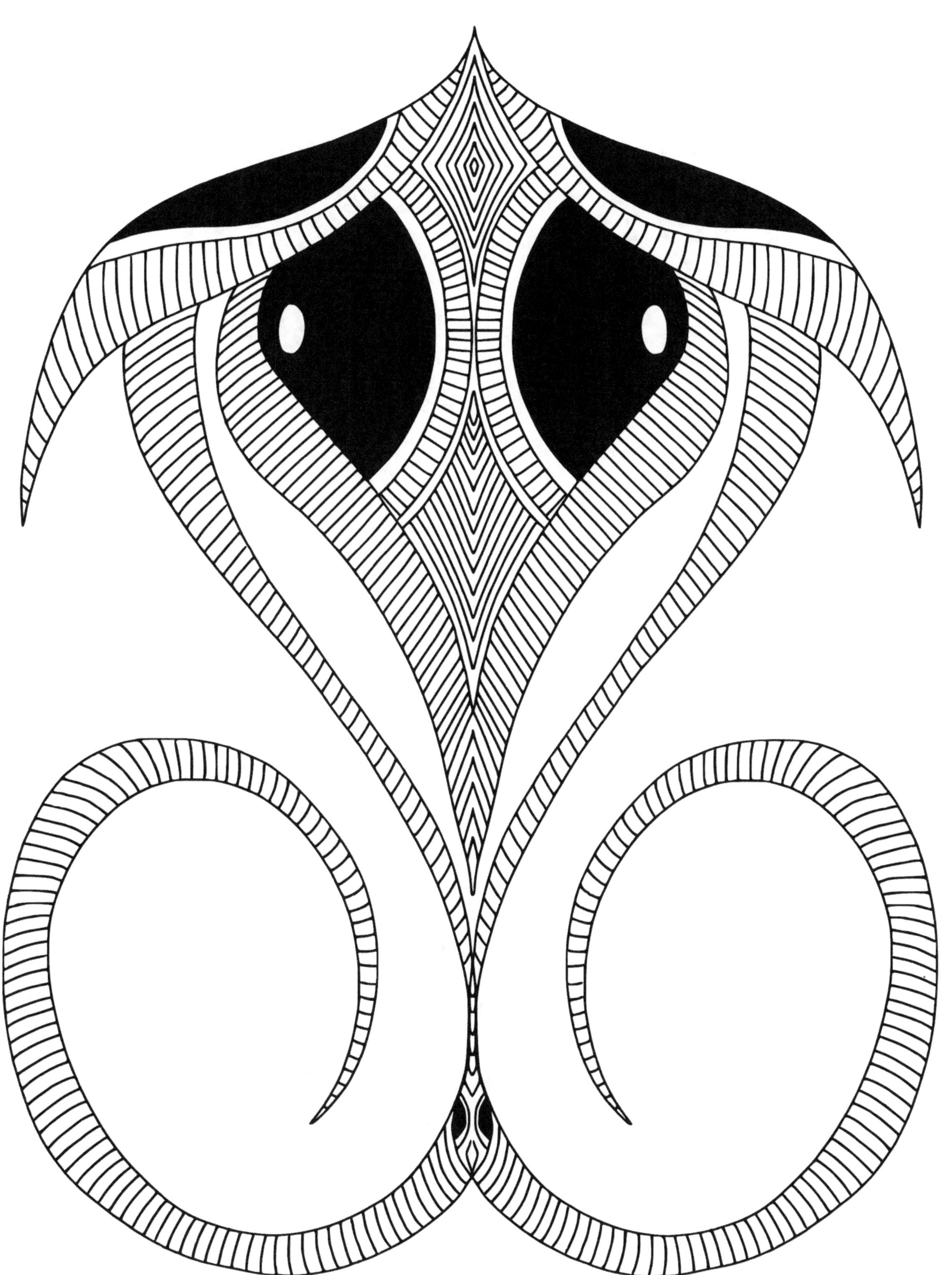

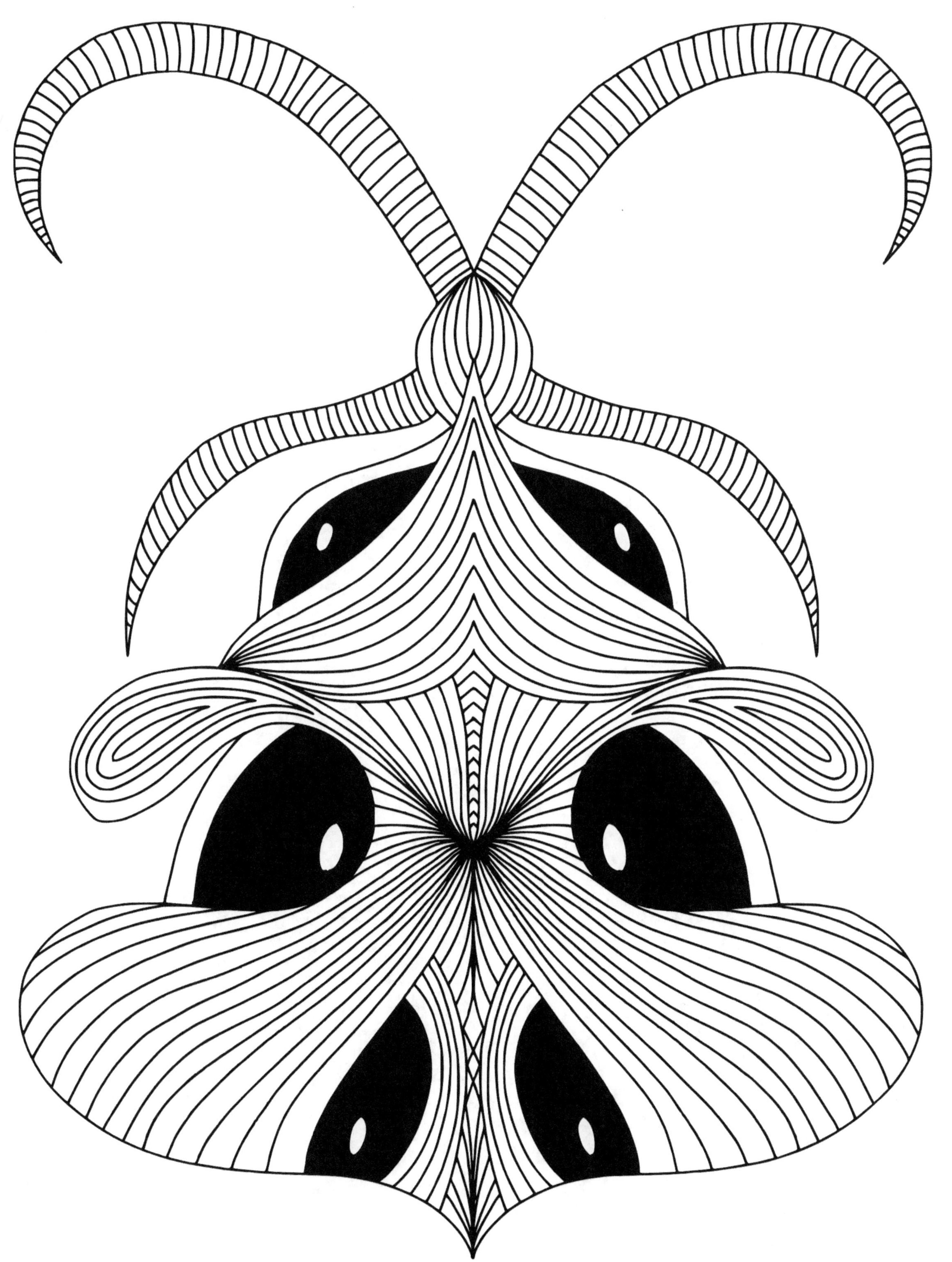

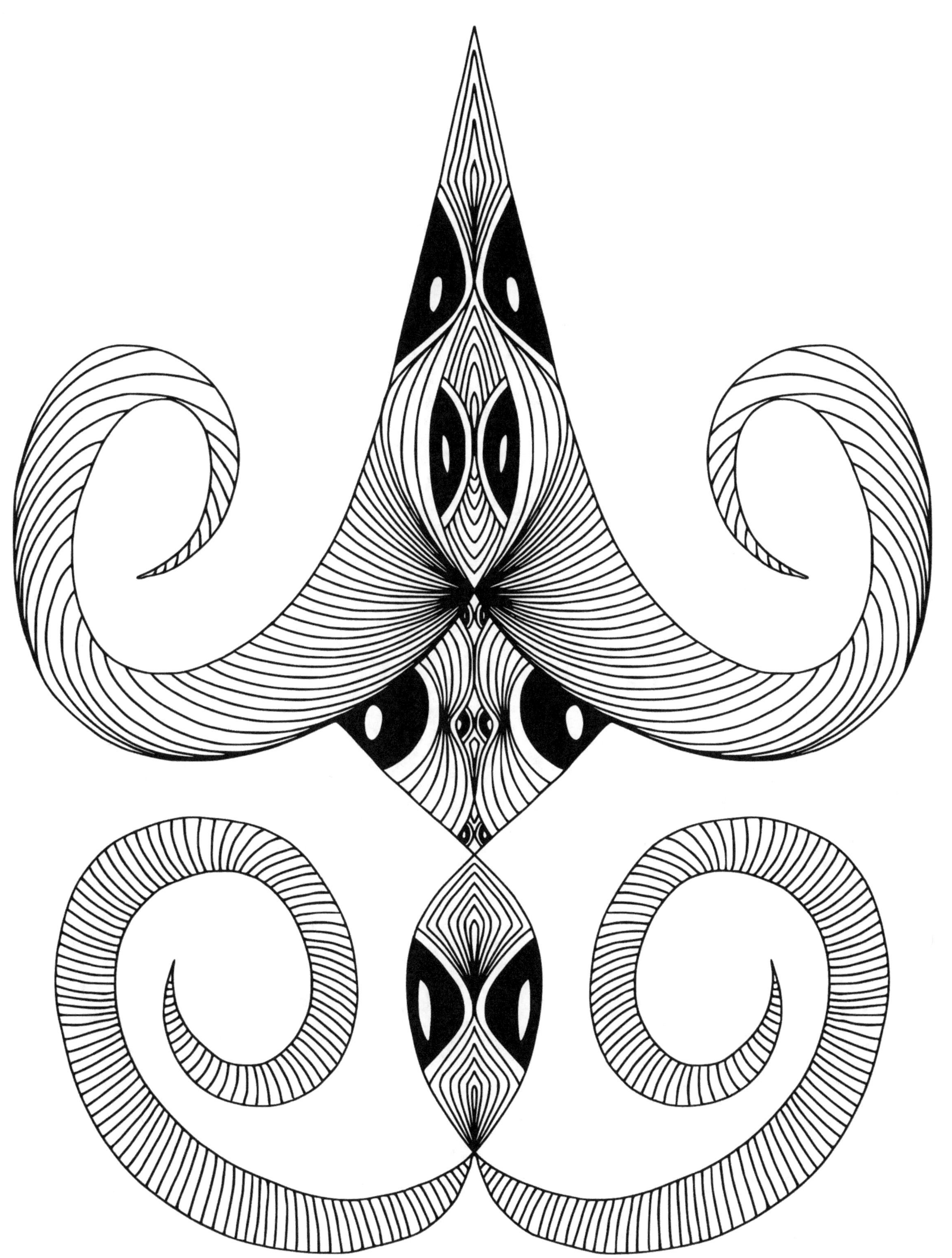

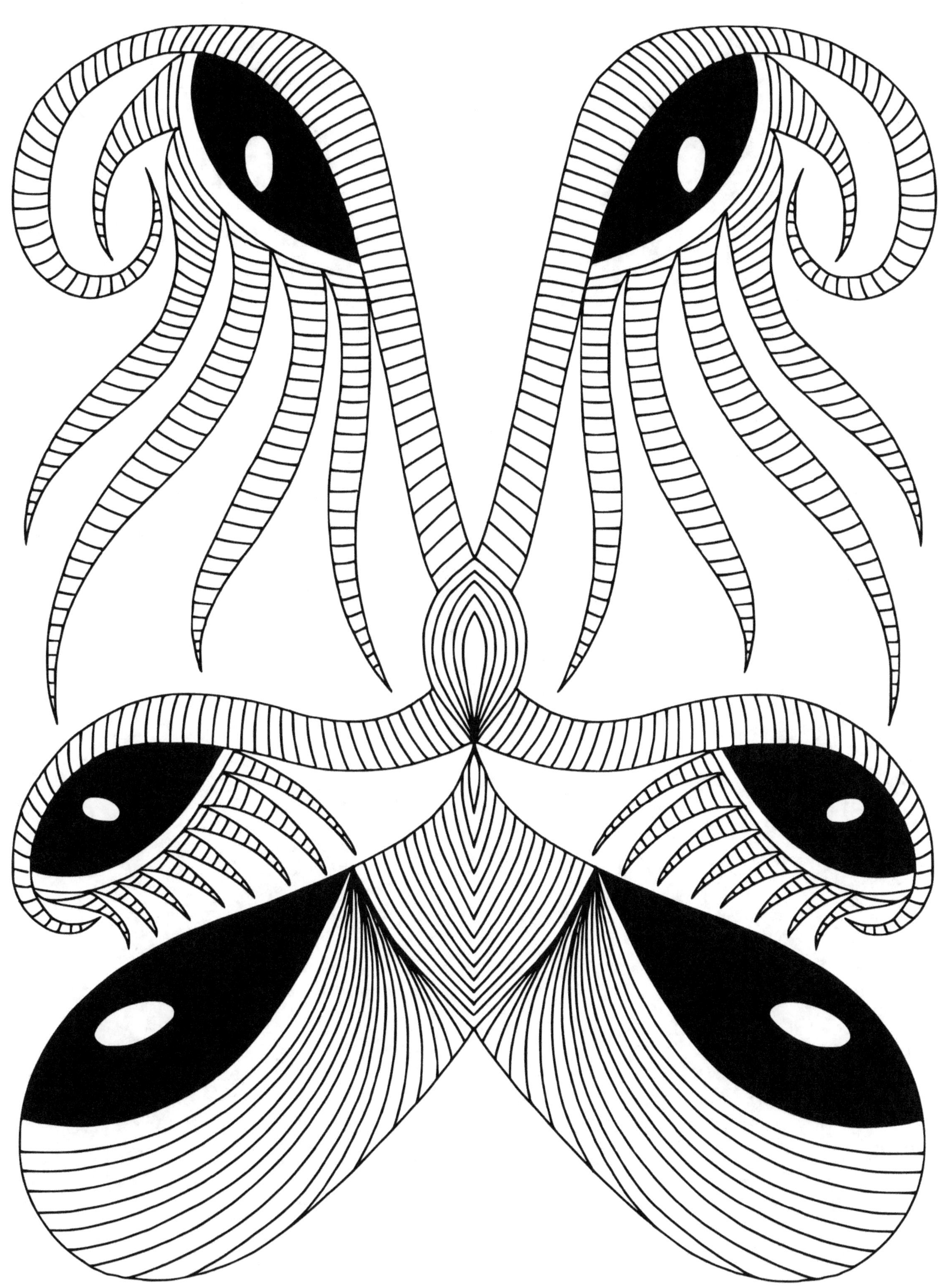

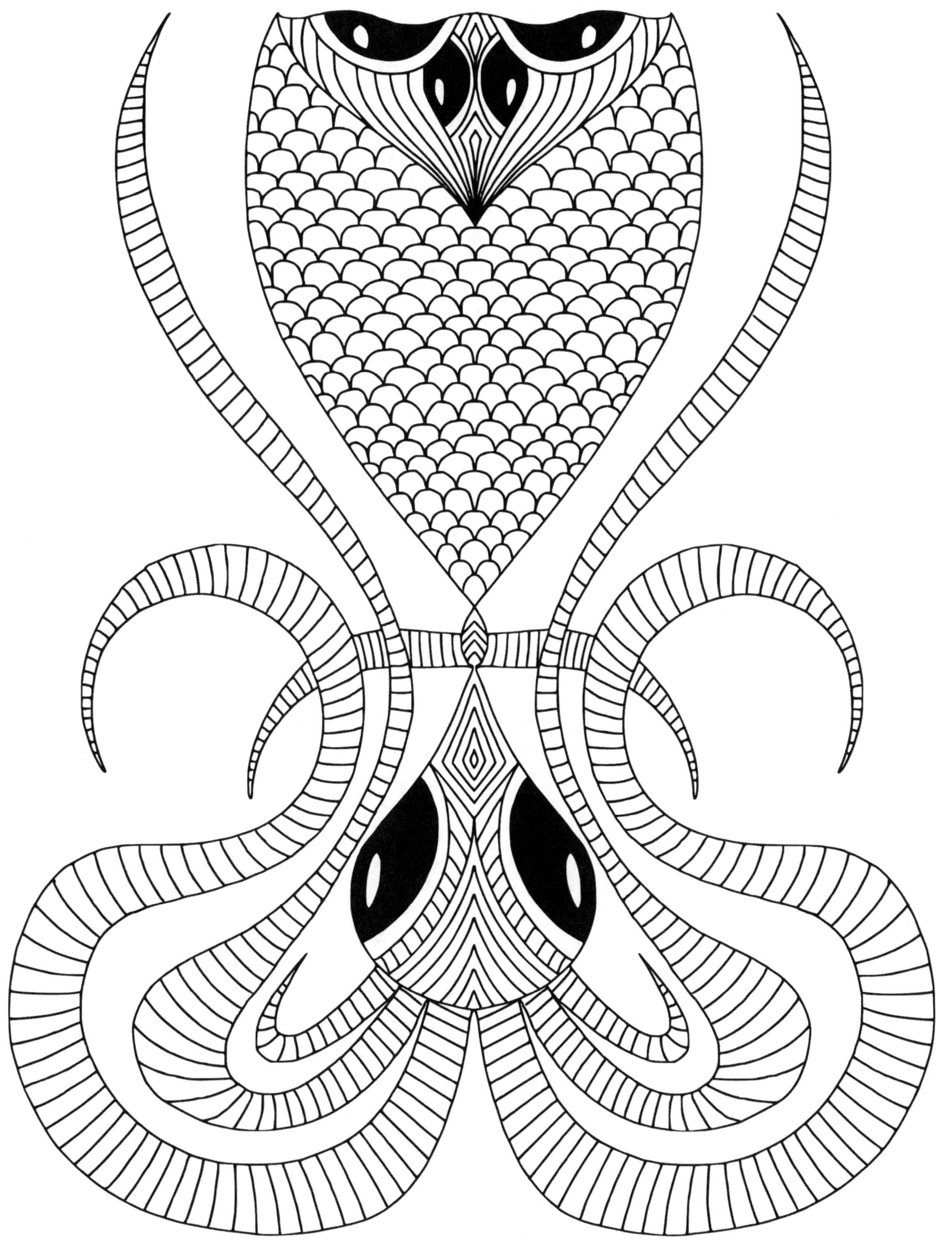

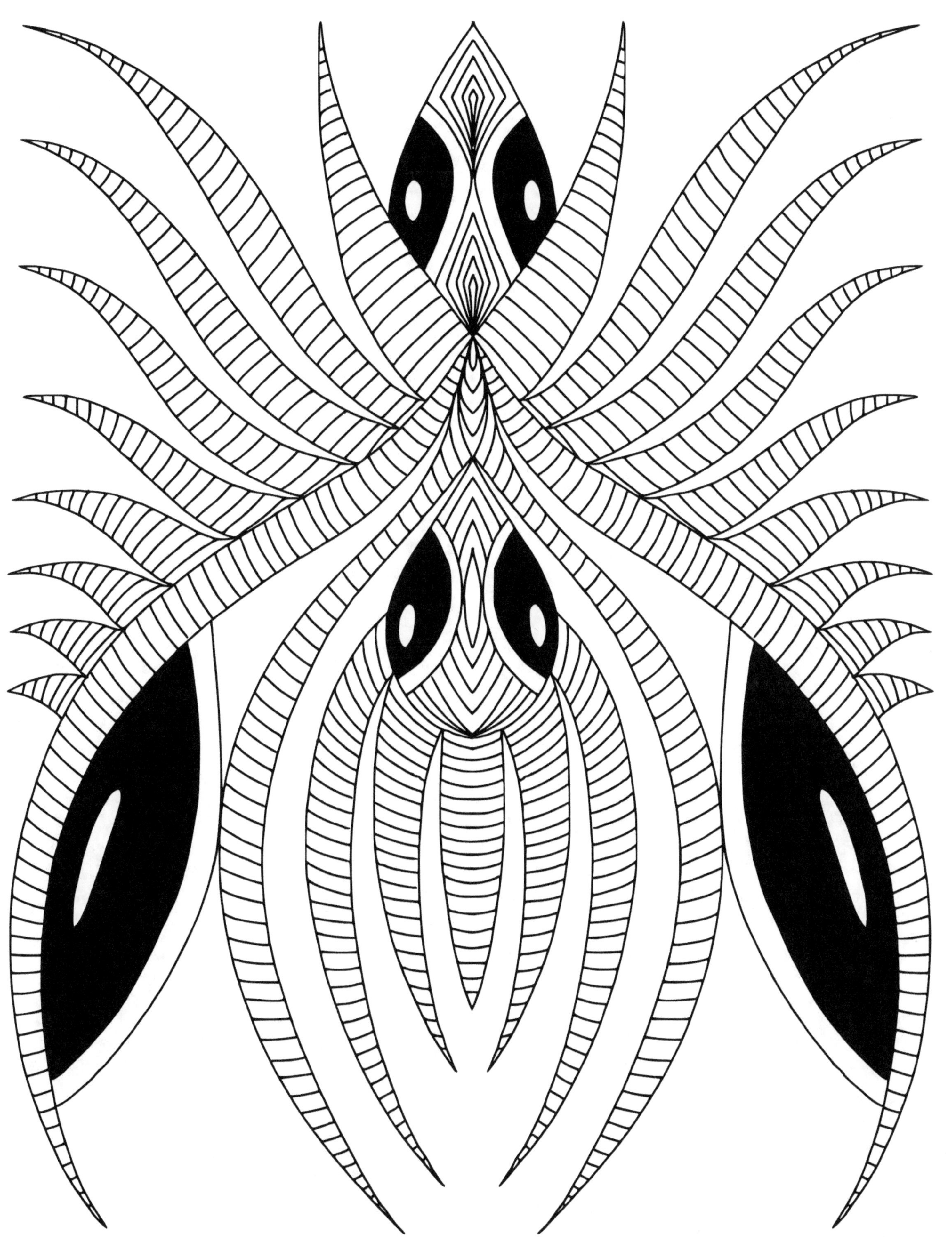

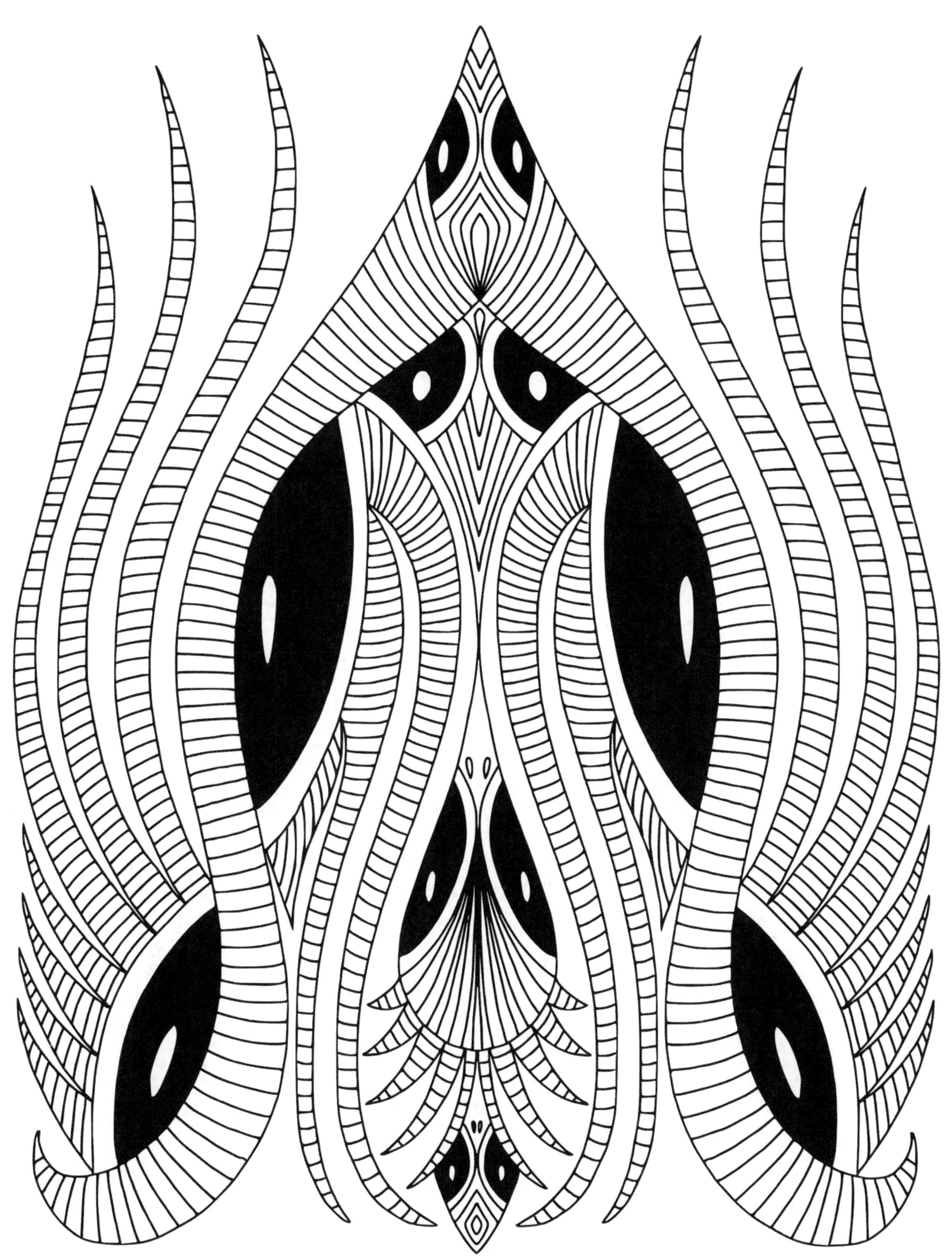

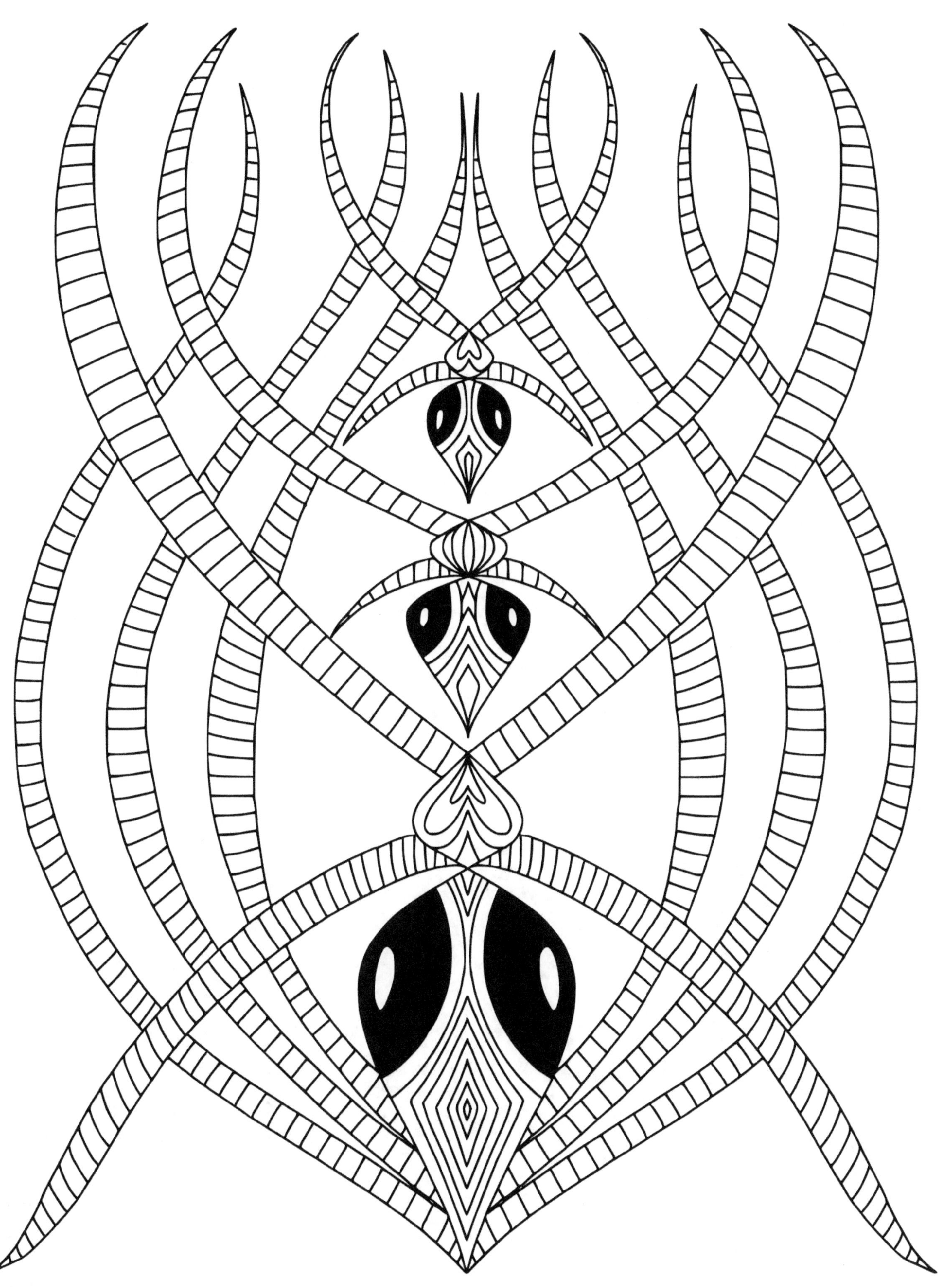

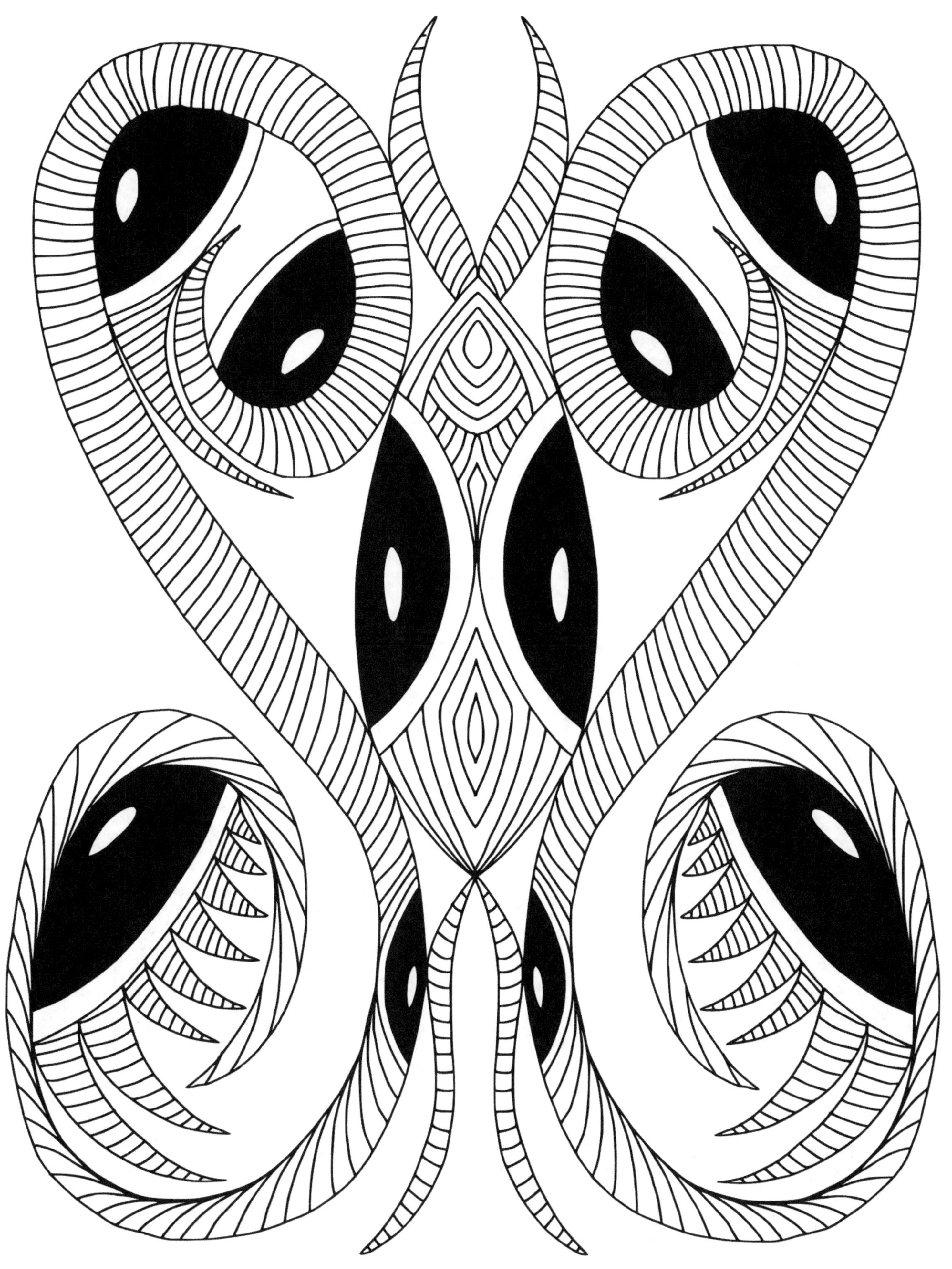

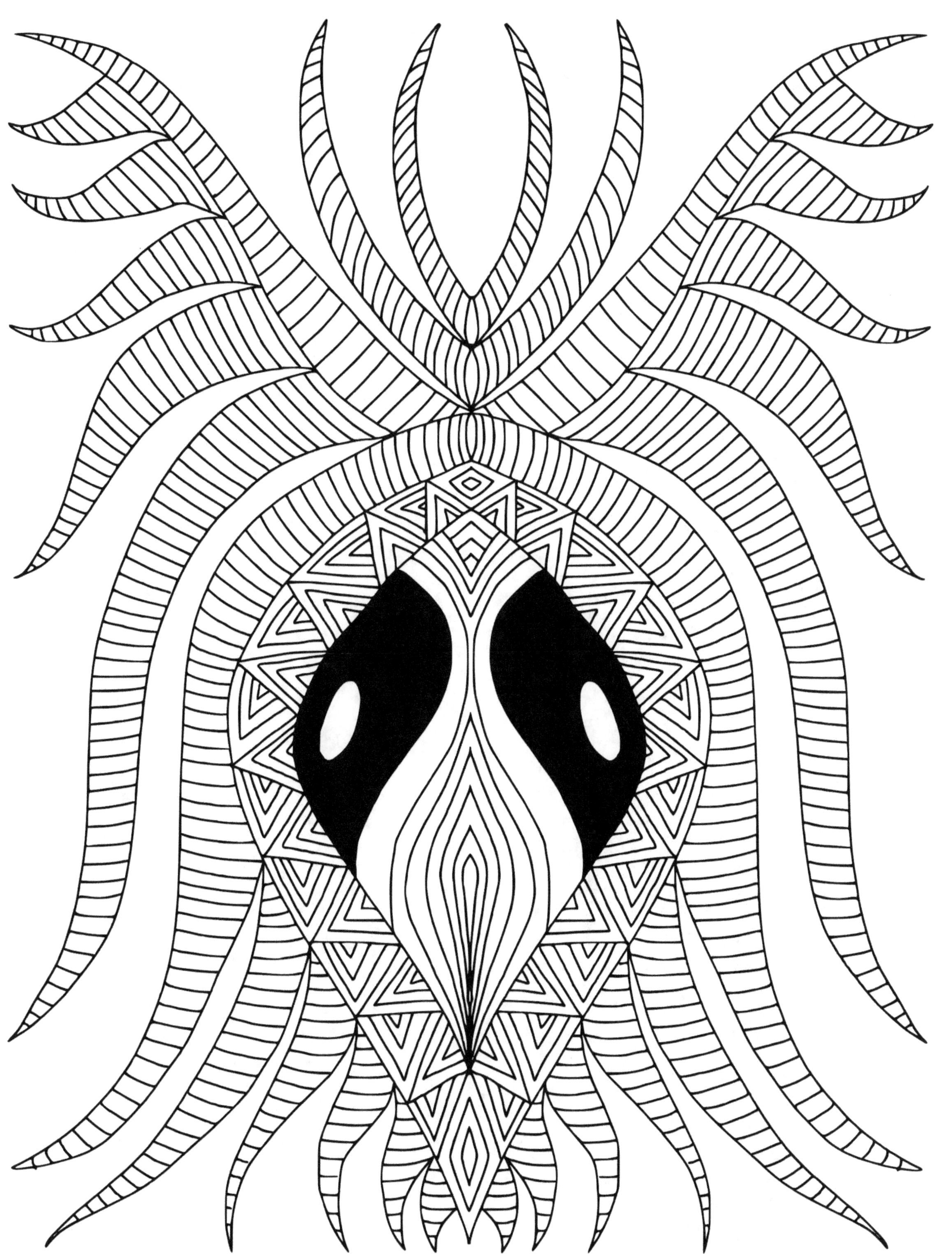

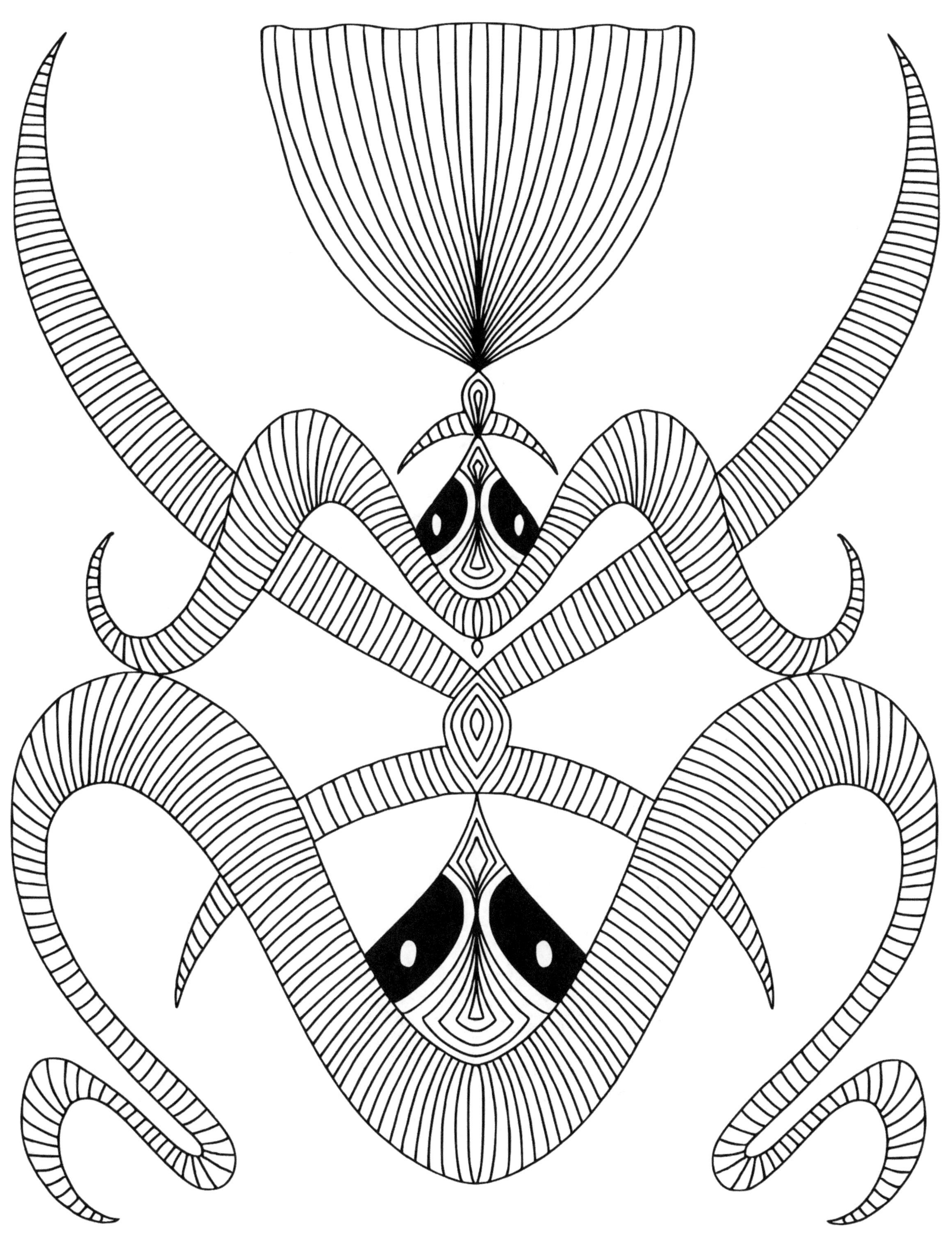

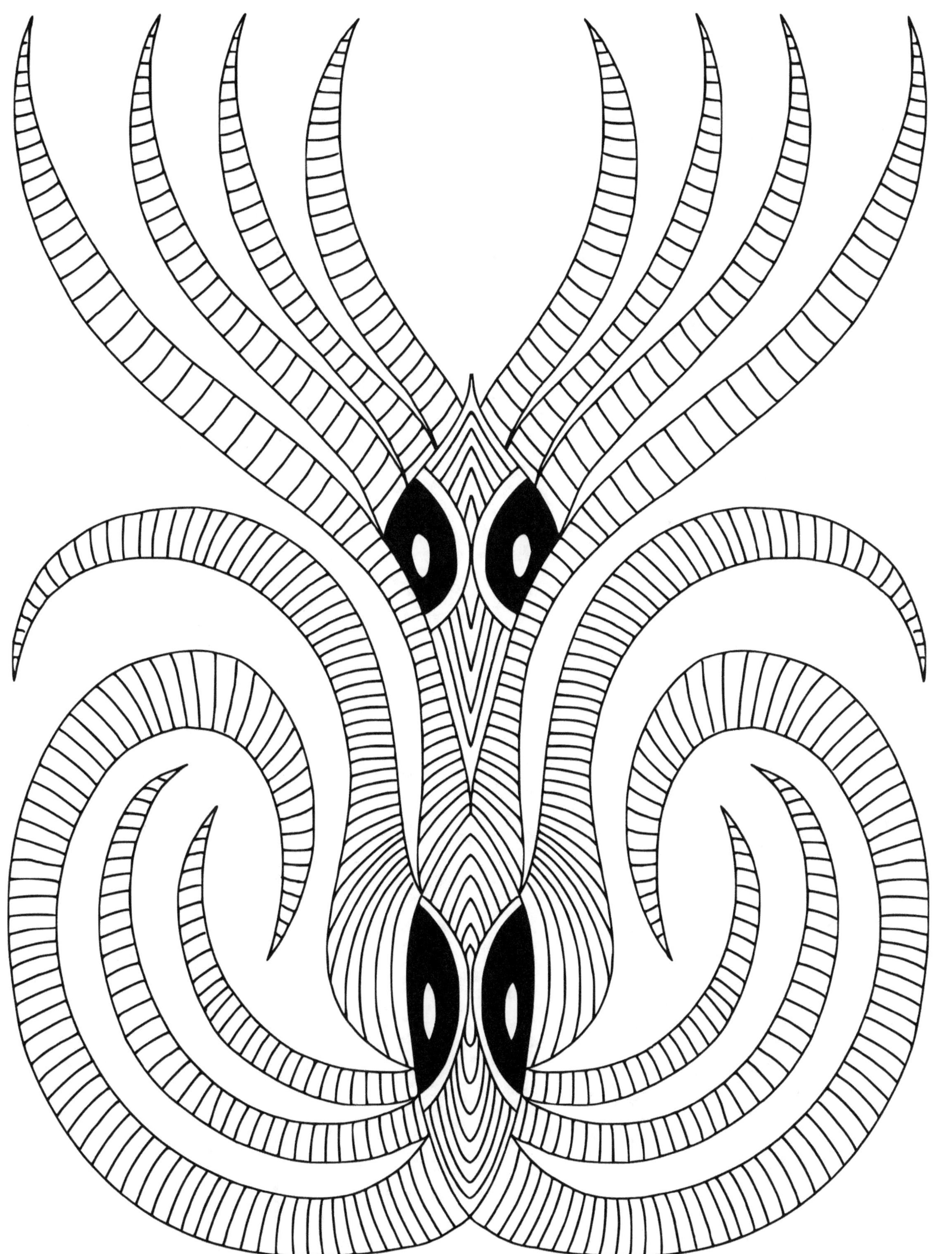

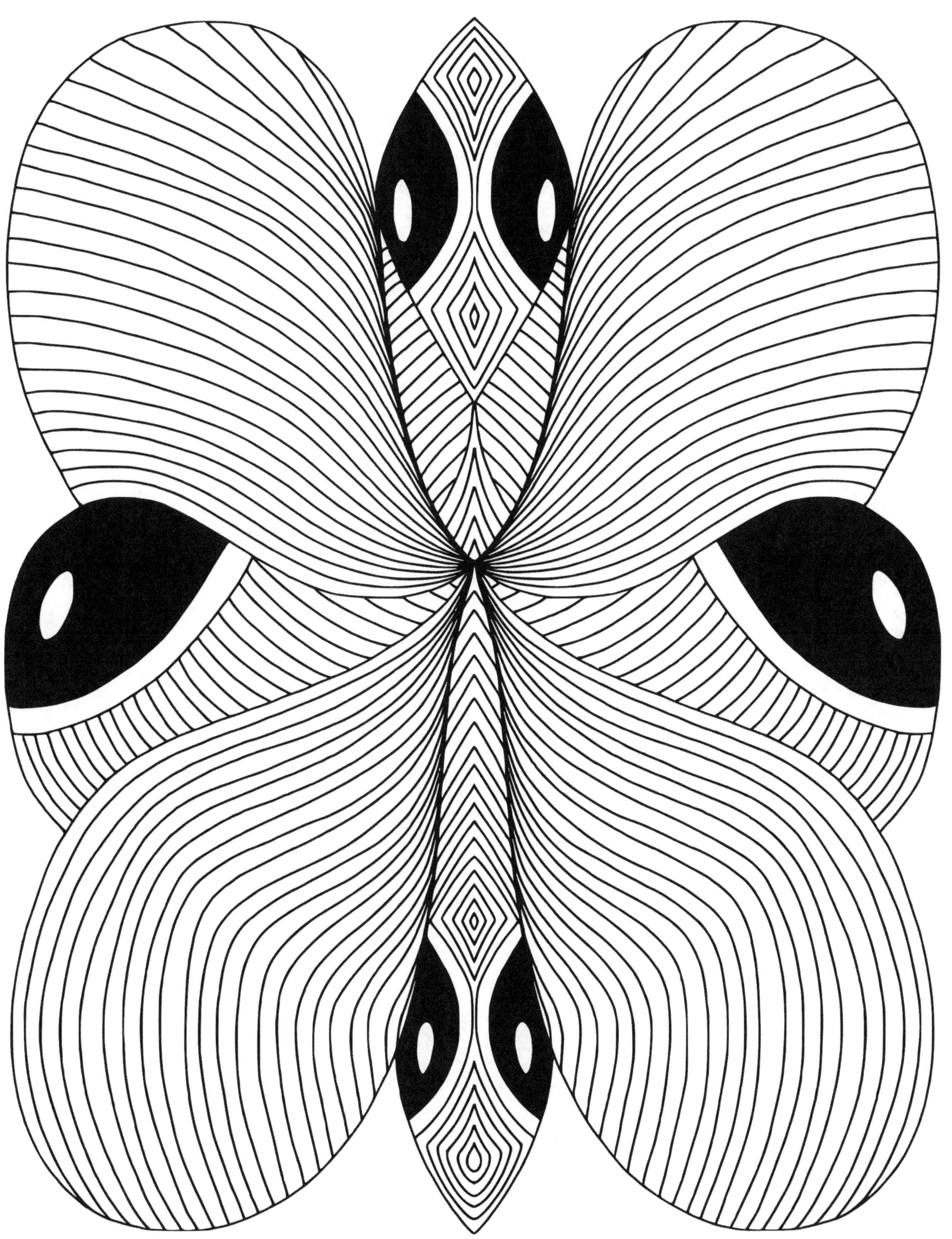

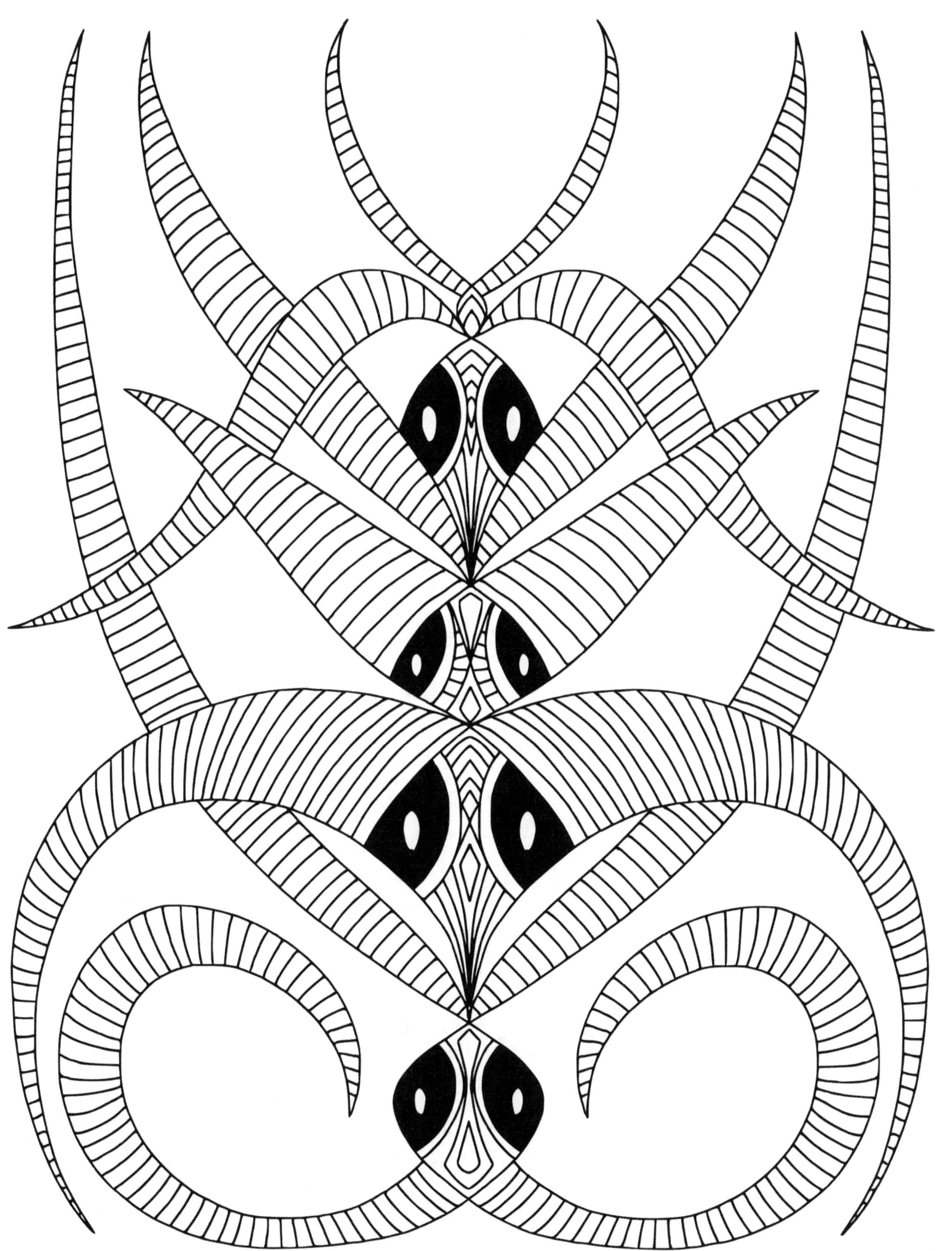

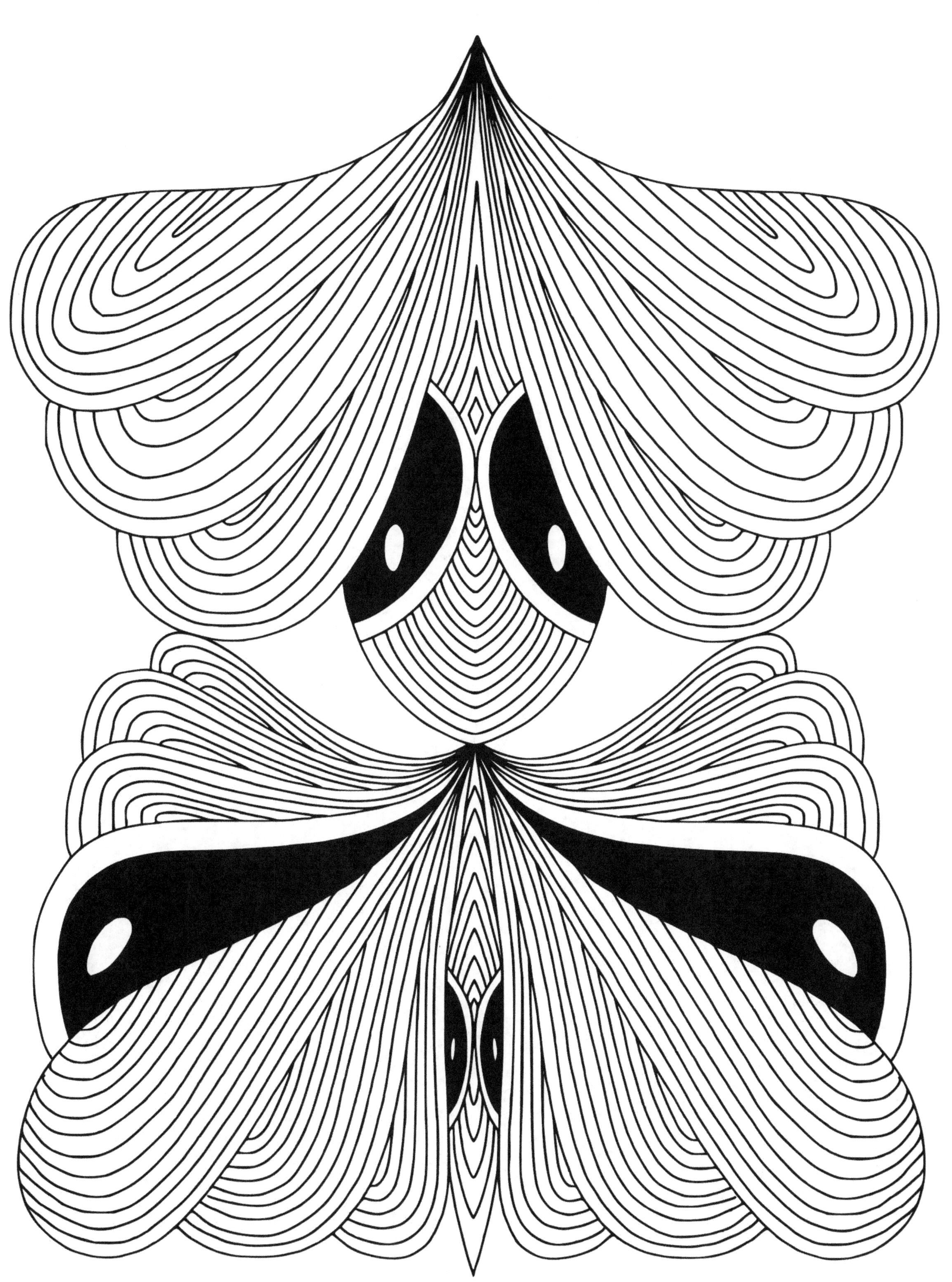

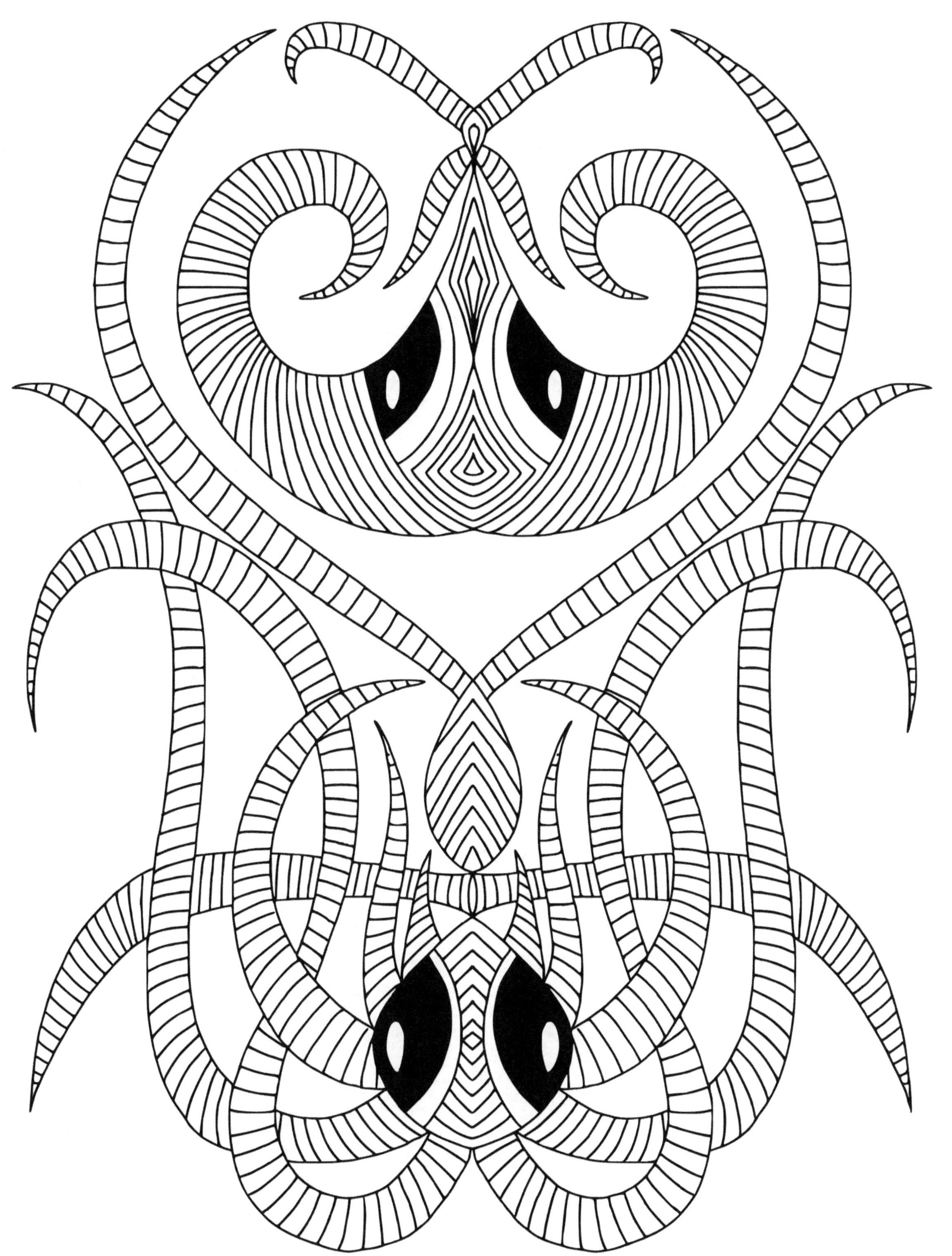

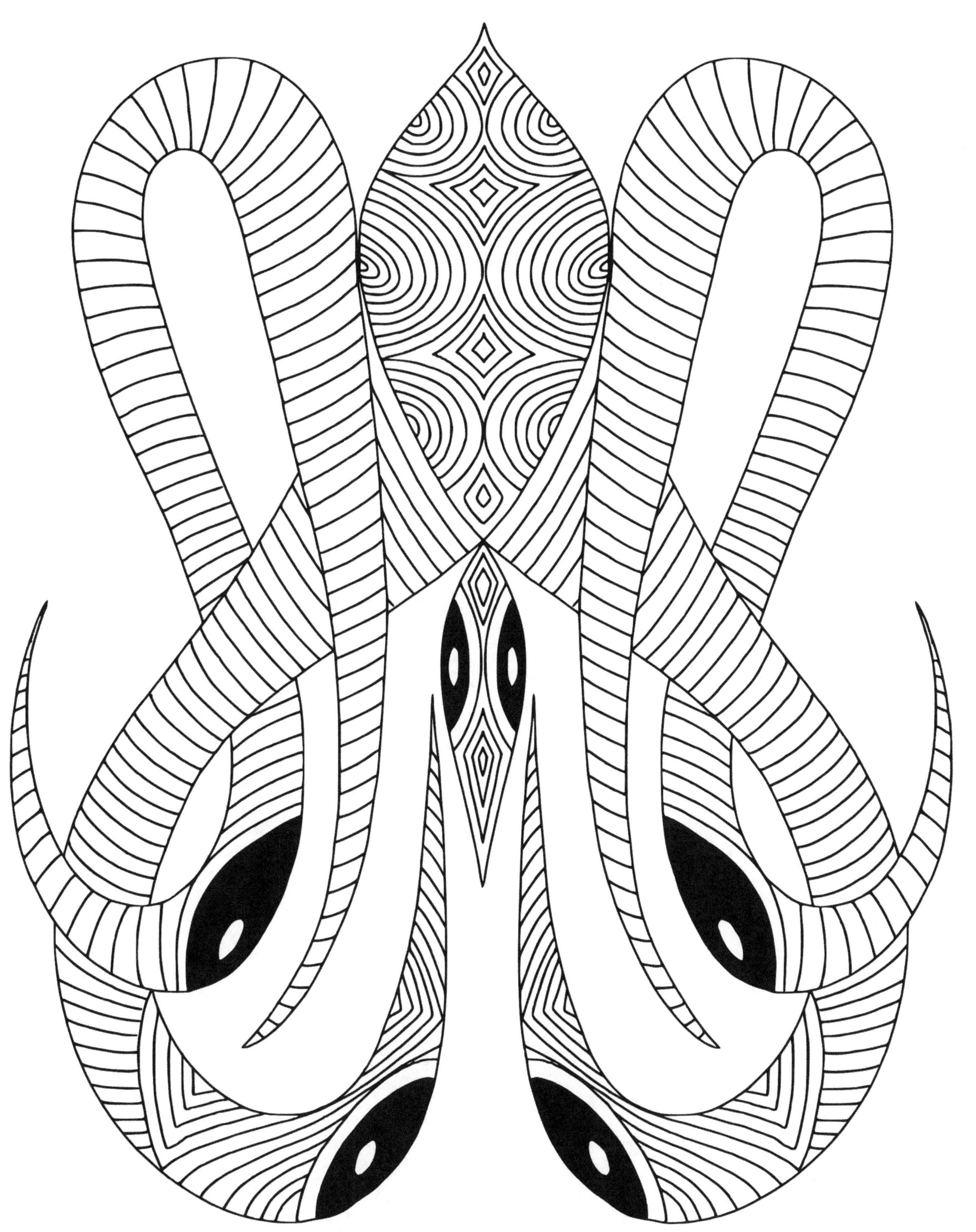

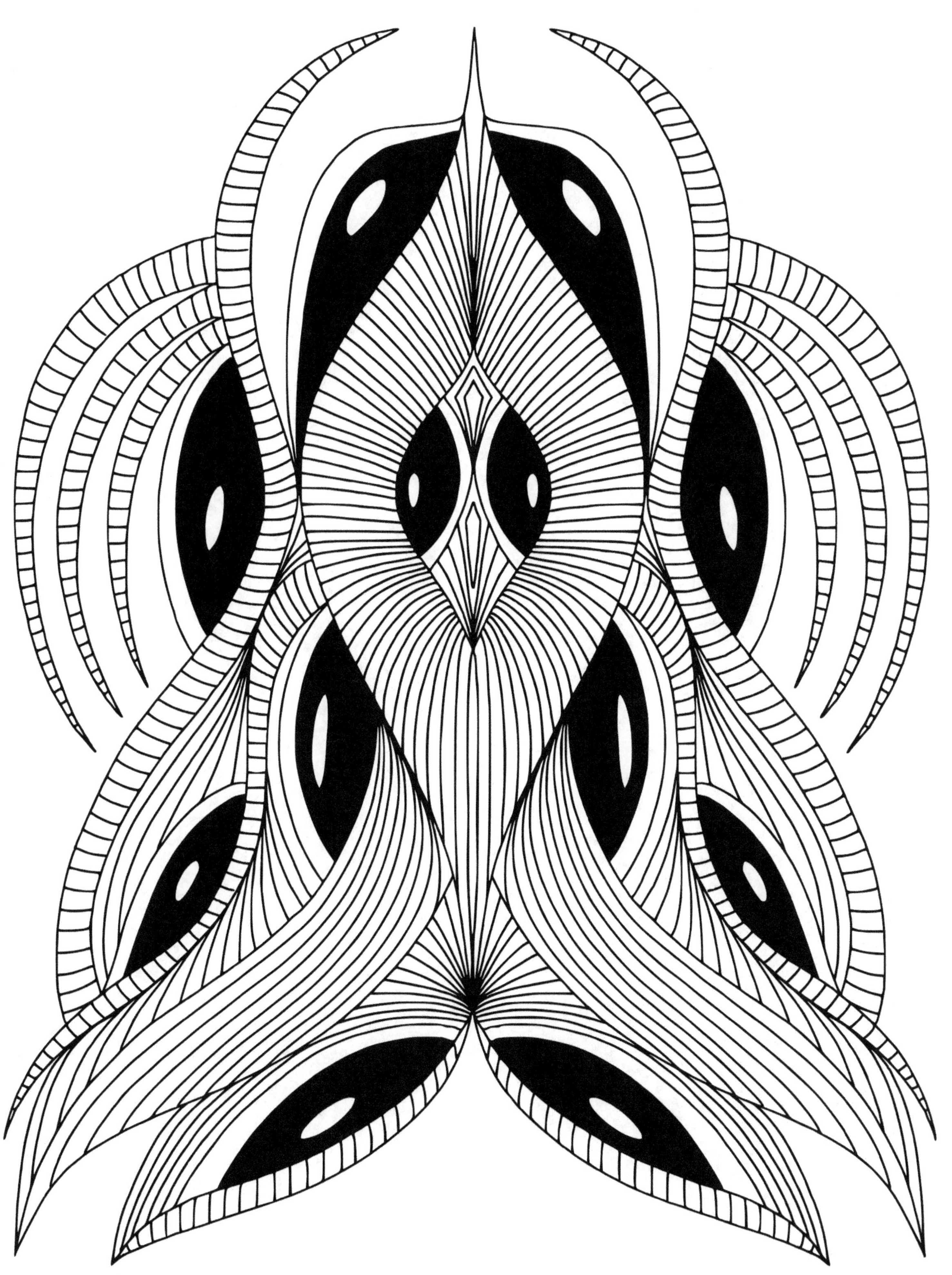

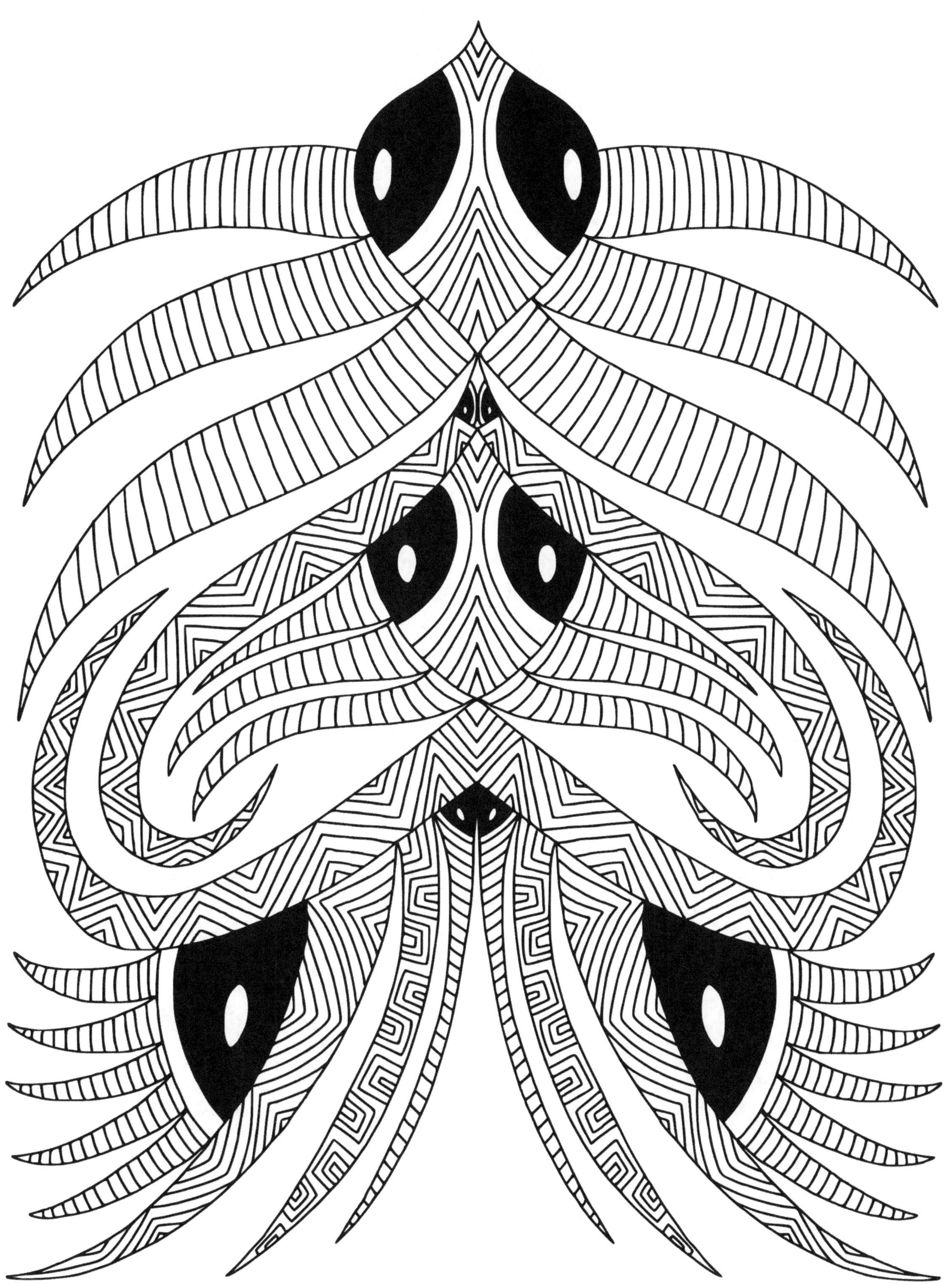

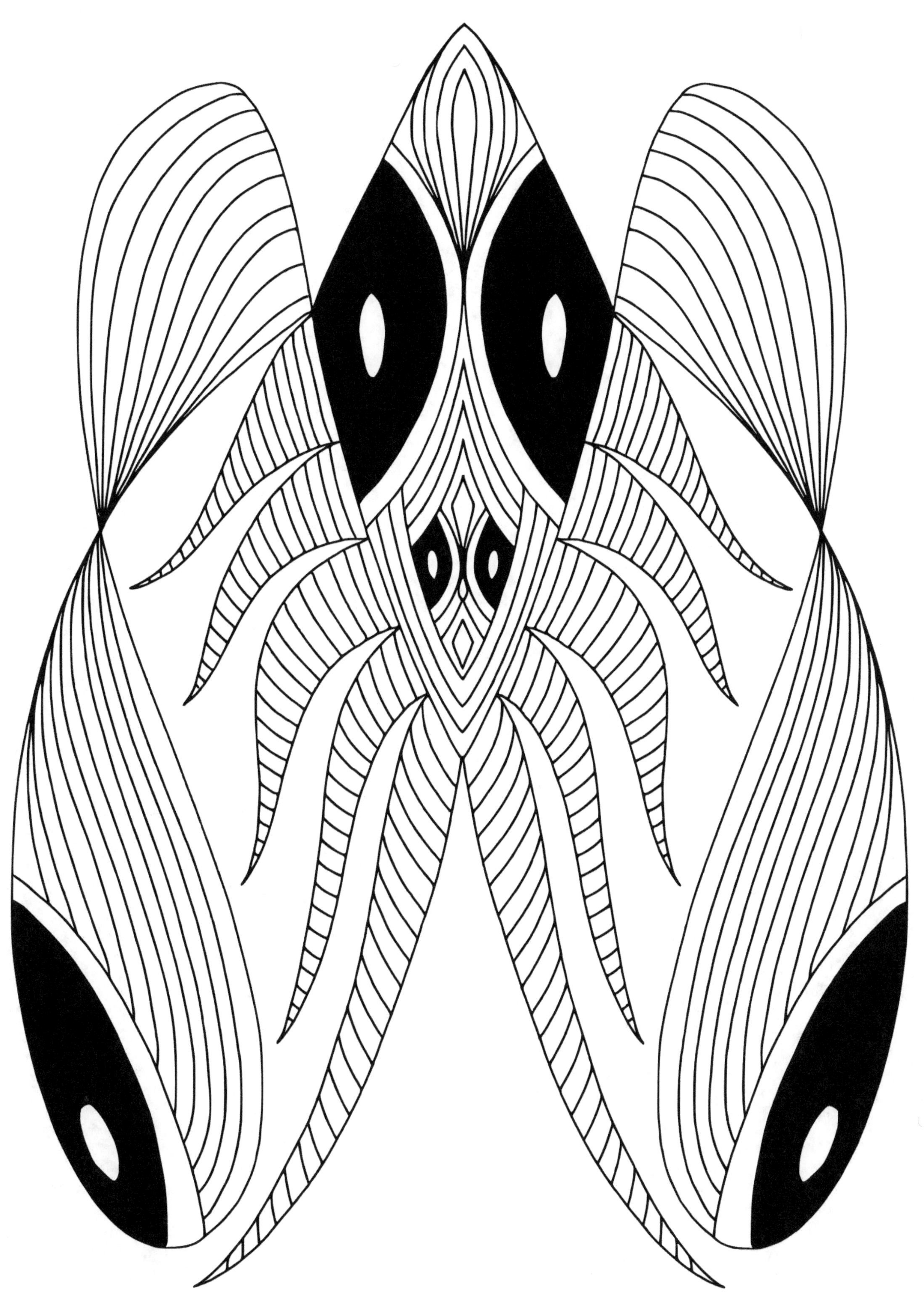

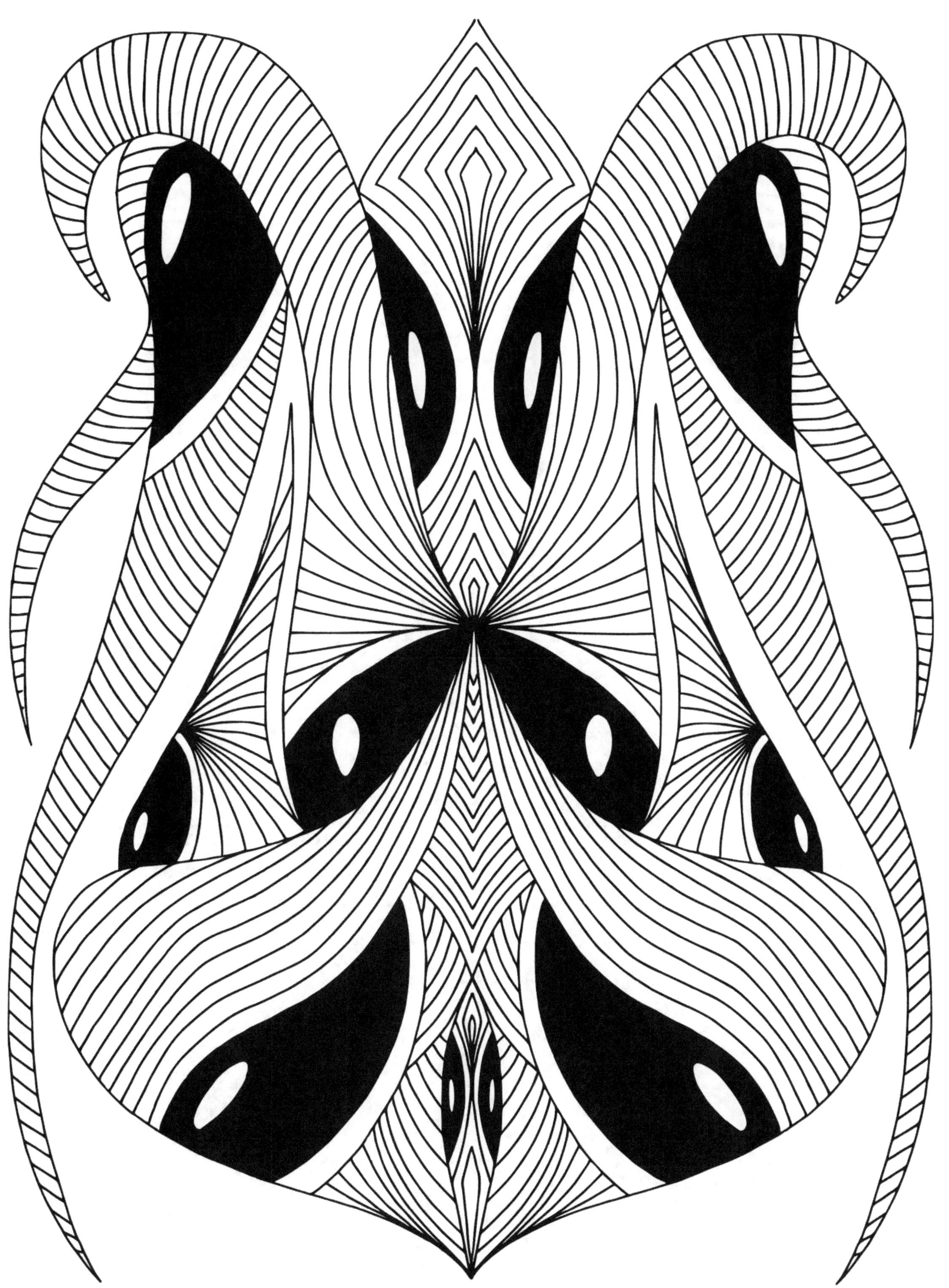

Test your colors here on the samples from
"My Pocket Coloring Companion"
&
"My Coloring Companion"

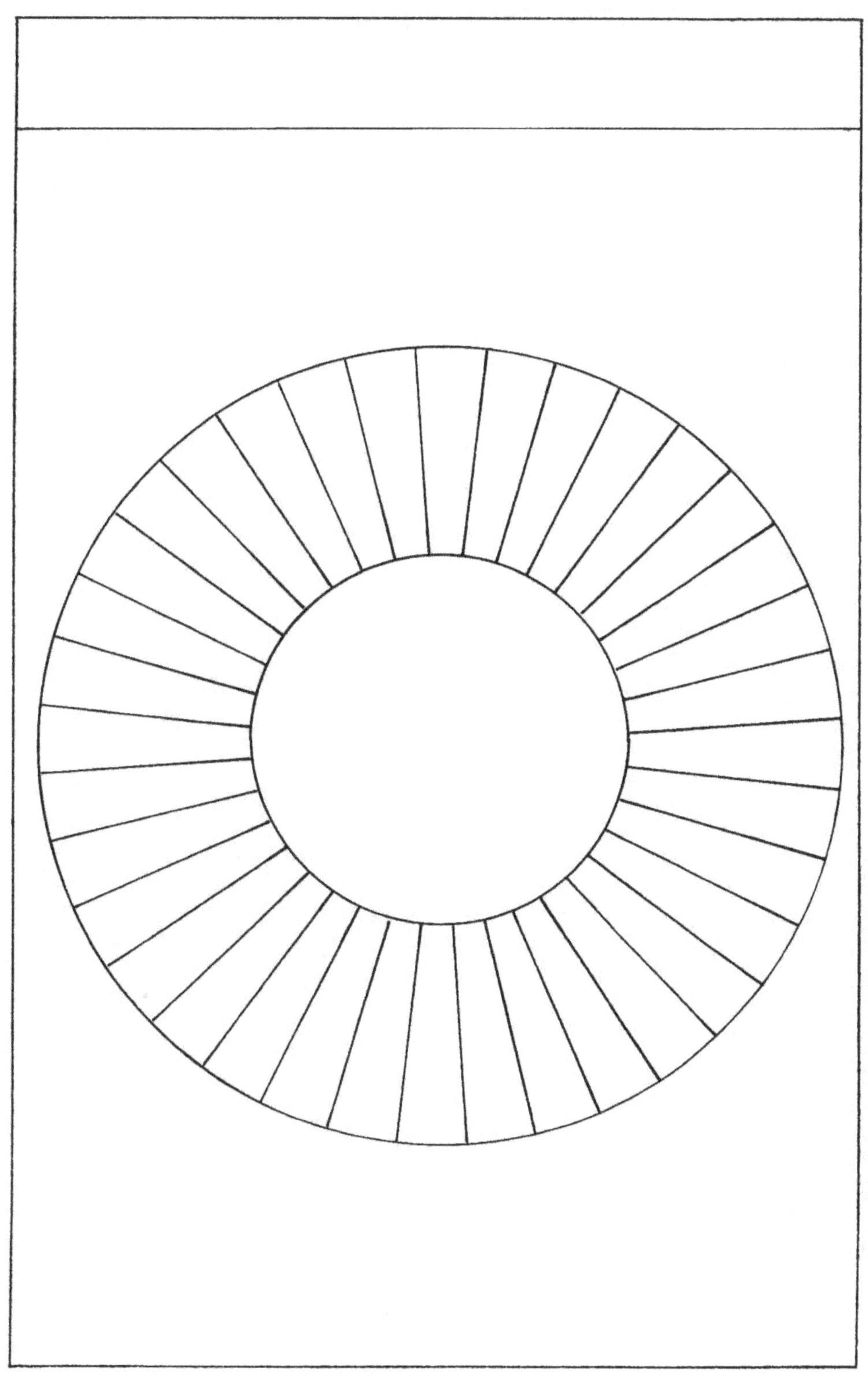

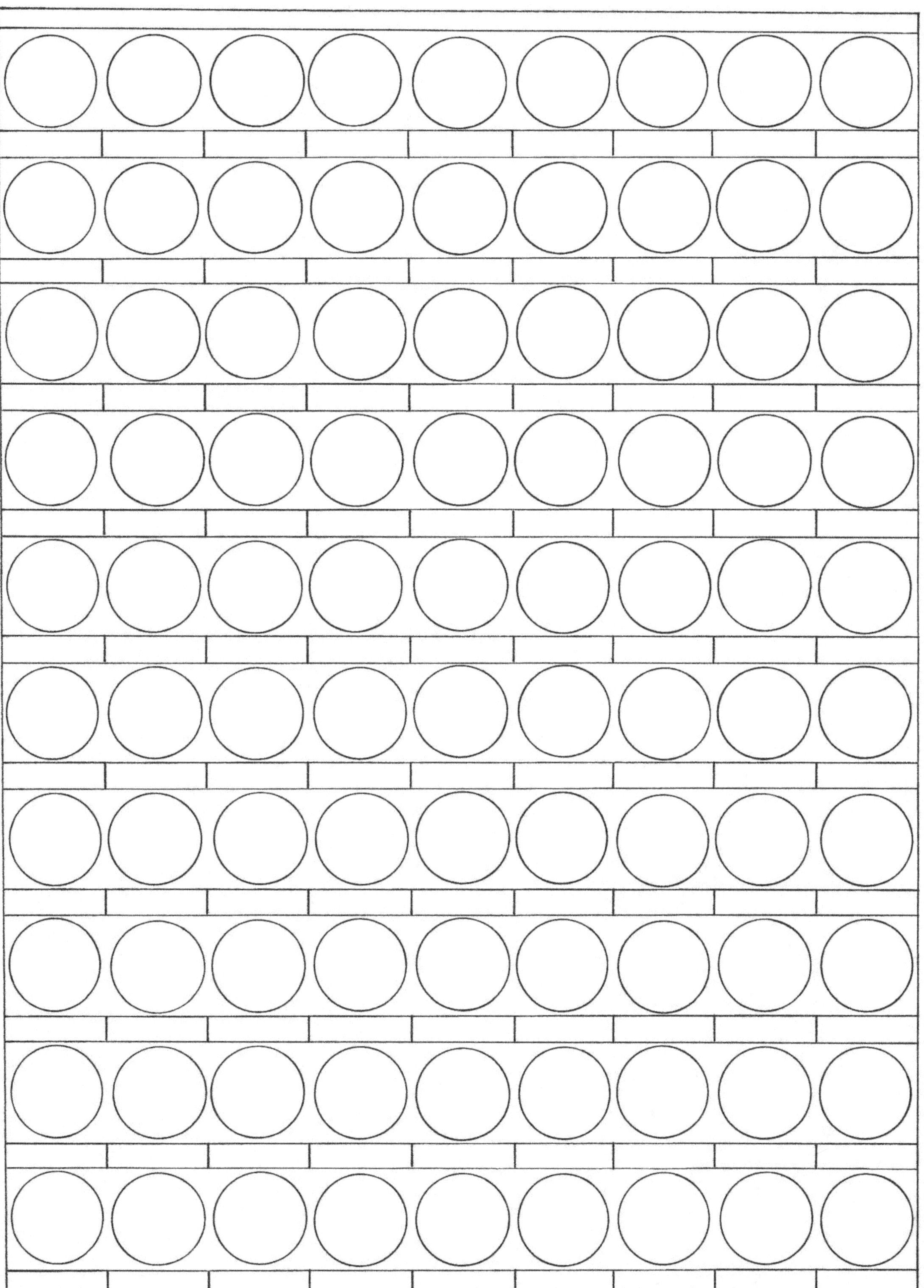

www.ingramcontent.com/pod-product-compliance
Lightning Source LLC
LaVergne TN
LVHW080607200726
843509LV00007B/264